FOOD
for the
SOUL

LUCY LORD

FOOD
for the
SOUL

Over 80 Delicious Recipes to Help You Fall Back in Love with Cooking

INTRODUCTION

food for thought

While I was writing this book, I thought a lot about what it is that I want to share. More than just pages of recipes sandwiched inside two covers, I'd like to help build connections through food, both between ourselves and the food we choose to eat, and ourselves and the people with whom we share our food, and our lives. More than just another cookbook, I'd like the recipes in this book to help you make changes in your day-to-day life for the better, from redefining your fridge leftovers to encouraging you to be creative by trying new recipes, learning new skills and gaining the confidence to break the recipe rules. Whether you are rediscovering a relationship with food and creativity in the kitchen or finding joy in something that used to be a frustration and an inconvenience, I hope that within these pages you'll find recipes to support your chosen lifestyle.

There are very few things in life that bind human experience, but the common bond we all have as humans is the need for food to survive. For thousands of years, food has been at the centre of celebrations and communities and today food is still regarded as one of the most important factors in social gatherings, in everything from weddings and holidays to the office lunch meeting. Everybody needs to eat, but our perceptions of what we eat, how we eat and why we eat can be so drastically different. As the world, technology and the demands on our lives evolve, we've become much less connected to the ingredients that go into our food – it's become much more tied to convenience and ticking a box. What can I grab and go? What can I eat in the car on the way to work? What has the most protein? The fewest calories? What can stay in my bag all day? While there's nothing inherently wrong with food becoming more functional and fitting in around our busy days and lives or goals, what I began to notice in myself and what I've noticed in the world around me, is that it can negatively impact our relationship with food and the relationship we have with our kitchens and ourselves.

We live in an ever-evolving world where convenience is king and your favourite takeaway can arrive at your door within the hour, without you even having to move. Time is becoming more scarce: we consume our breakfast in a frantic rush to get out the door, our lunch whilst hunched over a desktop or scrolling through a phone, only to look down at an empty plate and realise we paid absolutely no attention and took little or no joy from what we ate. Feeling unsatiated or low in energy, we might mindlessly snack throughout the afternoon and when we finally do get home, dinner feels like a huge effort to our already exhausted selves. The food we bought last week has gone off in the fridge and it's so much easier to grab a takeaway or a ready meal than it is to have to think about what we want for dinner, let alone consider our partners or children. The meals that we prepped on Sunday will probably be soggy, unappetising and tasteless come Wednesday, gathering condensation in the back of the office fridge. The big-batch Bolognese recipe that we spent hours making will be great tonight and tomorrow – but we'll probably be bored with it by day four, eating the same recipe in the same way.

There's nothing wrong with a good takeaway and I cherish the evenings I choose to have them. No washing up and a meal I wouldn't usually cook, all washed down with a nice glass of wine – winner. I don't think there's anything wrong with reading packaging labels and understanding what's in our food, and a grab-and-go breakfast (sometimes lunch too) from a shop is sometimes the best choice we can make that day. Life and our responsibilities can feel really overwhelming sometimes, and there's simply not always the opportunity to sit down cross-legged and savour each bite with our eyes closed like some mindful muses may lead us to believe, but that doesn't mean that our days, meals and good intentions need to slip into turmoil at the first road bump.

reclaim your time, your kitchen and your taste buds!

What I'd like to help share in the pages of this book are options and tools for when we can and do have the opportunity and time for ourselves – whether we have 15 minutes or an hour to spare – to enjoy getting into the kitchen, or if it's a two-minute-smoothie in the morning or catching up with friends over a coffee on the weekend with a thick slice of toasted banana bread. I wanted to create recipes that are simple but special, so that the idea of getting into the kitchen isn't something that will take hours out of your day and leave a pile of washing up, only to have to repeat the process again tomorrow.

In this book I'm sharing recipes that I have created over the years; some for when I'm in a hurry and need something easy and quick in under 15 minutes for dinner, others for when I have a long, lazy self-indulgent Sunday morning. Some that I know I can leave in a slow cooker so it's ready when I get in and others that I can pull together from leftovers in the week to create a new meal that I can take with me when I'm travelling for work and away from a fridge or oven. If in doubt, I can always fall back on my freezer, something that I used to completely take for granted. I've created recipes that can be made one way and enjoyed several other ways to add

variety so that you can love your leftovers whilst reducing food waste (not to mention time, energy and money!), whether it's slow-cooked chicken stuffed into a bun as a slider with loads of lime-drenched guacamole, or piled on top of a thin, crispy pizza base with caramelised red onion and fresh, peppery rocket. Every ingredient and every recipe has a purpose behind it and, as much as possible, ingredients can be substituted, leaving you to create your own spin on recipes with a new-found confidence and creativity.

I like to encourage people to eat more mindfully and to enjoy food as an experience rather than something to fear, stress or worry about. I believe that in the same way that money is more likely to be mindlessly spent when it's been gifted or won, rather than earned through time and work (over 70 per cent of people who win the lottery go bankrupt within a few years), when we spend time and effort creating our meals in the kitchen, we're more likely to take the time to enjoy them, as well as being more conscious of the ingredients, time and energy that goes into our food. See page 18 for more on mindful eating.

falling back in love with food

Creating recipes has taught me several lessons that I try to carry with me through day-to-day life: to stay curious, to try new things, to always question what I think I know or what I'm told, to persevere when things go wrong (which is inevitable and frequent!) and to have the ability to 'fail forward' and learn from my mistakes. I love the trial and error of recipe building as much as I love the one-try wonders; the recipes where everything that you've planned on paper, from the textures to colours and tastes, comes together even better than you imagined, as well as those that go horribly, horribly wrong and sometimes take days – if not weeks – of going back to square one until you're happy with them. You don't learn an awful lot when things always go right, so being able to take these lessons, learning curves and recipes to pass on and share through life has always been something I've loved about cooking.

I didn't step foot in a kitchen until my early twenties. I'm grateful that my mum was a great cook but when I left home for university when I was 17, I thrived on convenience food and quick fixes: three-sugar milky teas, three-scoop instant coffees, cans of energy drinks, KFC, McDonald's and sugary cereals from midday through to midnight. All the snacks that weren't available at home – crisps, chocolate and sugary drinks – became my staples. After graduating and moving to a new city on my own, I decided to take more control in the kitchen in an attempt to shift some of the weight I'd gradually gained at university. It started with the 'ready-to-cook' supermarket ranges that are all prepared for you – just put them in the oven and try not to forget about them. Soon I discovered that I enjoyed my new-found time in the kitchen and slowly began experimenting and creating, making food as gifts and things to bring to occasions. I learned the long and hard way about food preparation and what did and didn't survive living in a handbag all day. Work generally involved long hours with no access to a fridge or microwave and lots of travel time spent in a car. I'm passionate now about creating recipes that really support a busy lifestyle rather than hinder it; it should be one less thing to worry about, not an additional strain on our already long to-do lists.

Somewhere along the road of my early-days experimenting, I stumbled into the realms of 'clean eating', paleo, IIFYM (If It Fits Your Macros), cheat meals and all of the other ways that the wellness and fitness industries began to dress up food restriction. Breakfast would be a dry and chalky protein pancake mix drowning in zero-calorie syrup and suddenly it was #science to have butter and coconut oil in coffee, every cake mix had scoops of protein powder added and chocolate mousse was made with avocados and egg whites. No 'health kick' would be right without at least five miserable days spent juicing fruits and vegetables, and it took several trips to different food shops to get the weird and wonderful ingredients needed for a paleo cheesecake, often costing a small fortune. I began to see food as 'good 'or 'bad' and entered the all too familiar restriction–binge cycle. I fell out of love with food and in the process, I fell out of love with myself.

I left the UK to move to Sydney and spend some time travelling. New countries, new flavours and new experiences began to ignite the love for food that I had lost, and slowly, over the years, I began to rebuild both my understanding and relationship around food. The kitchen became a creative space again and meals became an experience, without the negative connotations around food.

My goal is to make simple, good food accessible to everybody. To remove the elitism that sometimes comes from 'eating well' and the concept that it takes a lot of time, money or fridge space to do so. I want to emphasise balance and the freedom, joy and connection that food can bring to our lives. Living well and eating well looks different to everyone. I don't believe in discriminating against foods; nothing is good or bad. We have at least three opportunities a day – that's 21 a week, 84 a month and 1,092 a year – to enjoy food. I want to help people enjoy as many of them as possible.

KEY TO SYMBOLS

 vegetarian

 vegan

 dairy free

 gluten free

start the day right

How you spend your morning determines the quality of your day, which determines the quality of your life. The importance of what we choose to consume to start our days stretches far beyond what goes on our plates; it's also about what we watch, what we read and what we listen to. Reaching for your phone first thing in the morning can be tempting (up to 80 per cent of people do this) but research shows that it increases stress and anxiety and decreases our ability to focus on tasks for the rest of the day, making us more likely to engage in distracting habits such as more phone scrolling and mindless snacking. Likewise, it can be tempting to eat breakfast on the go on the way to work or slumped over our desktops when we get into the office, rather than making time to sit down and enjoy it. But preparing or buying grab-and-go food does not mean you have to literally eat it on the go; finding time to sit down – even for five minutes on a park bench – to really enjoy your food not only increases satiety but introduces a brief moment of stillness in what can otherwise be a chaotic morning. The University of Harvard found that eating while distracted (in the car, on a phone or laptop or while watching TV) not only increased the amount of food we consumed at that sitting, but also throughout the rest of the day. Not reaching for my phone first thing in the morning and making time to sit down to breakfast, undistracted – whether that's at home, in a work environment or while travelling – have been by far two of the hardest habits for me to build, but two of the most beneficial. I have devoted a whole chapter to my favourite 'breakfast' recipes, to be enjoyed at any time of the day. See page 36.

think inside the (Tupperware) box

Learning to cook is only one piece of the puzzle. Unless you're making absolutely everything from scratch for every meal (I am yet to meet such people), food storage is such an important component. Even the best salads, tastiest meals and delicious bakes can turn to shit if they are not stored effectively.

Choosing farmers' markets usually ensures a fresher product (that therefore lasts longer) but if you are buying your fresh produce from a supermarket, make sure you always root around at the back for the stuff with the longest use-by dates. Discounted fruit and veg can be a great purchase, although they're usually on their way out, so make sure you use them as soon as possible, otherwise you'll end up throwing them away and losing money – even if you saved some in the short term.

Always let any hot foods completely cool before storing, otherwise expect condensation (and when popping off the lid on a packed lunch to be greeted with a small rainstorm).

Storage containers

Not all food-storage containers are created equal and investing in a good collection will save you time, money and waste in the future. My favourite are glass ones with an airtight 'snap and lock' sealed lid. Fridge, freezer, oven and microwave safe, you can see what's inside, they're easy to clean, are dishwasher friendly and don't 'stain' like their plastic counterparts. They are widely available in a range of sizes and styles in supermarkets and online, so you won't have to break the bank to invest in a good set. I really like the stainless-steel bento boxes with in-built sections to keep foods separate for salads; and for larger storage boxes that won't be exposed to heat (to store pasta, for example), BPA-free plastic ones are a good choice and much more affordable and practical.

A lot of takeaways are moving towards recyclable or compostable food containers (such as BioPak) but if you do have leftover plastic containers, clean them out and reuse and recycle them. I'll sometimes use them either to store my herbs in the fridge, or for things like piping nozzles and baking decorations. Many ziplock bags can be safely washed and reused for five years or more. Always reuse and recycle where possible and avoid single-use materials.

Kitchen paper

I always have a roll of kitchen paper in my kitchen! Some food-storage containers come with a removable raised grate at their base – this is to keep air circulating freely and stop foods from becoming soggy. If you don't have one of these contraptions, using a folded piece of kitchen paper under anything that can release moisture is a great hack – think frittatas, pastries, savoury muffins and most baked goods. Folded kitchen paper baskets are great for separating nuts and seeds from the rest of a salad, breakfast, curry or soup – keeping them crisp and crunchy. Remove when you're ready to eat and use the kitchen paper as a napkin. They're also useful to help keep salad bags and herbs fresh for weeks (see pages 58–9).

Keeping things hot or cold

I've worked in a whole range of climates, from 45°C+ in the Australian outback to -10°C in Scottish winters, for most of my career, often with no access to a fridge or any way to heat food up, so I've done my fair share of trialling suitable packed lunches! Often, I'd have to pack all my meals for the whole day, as remote locations or time constraints usually meant that stopping at a café or even a service station for food was out of the question. Endless packets of crisps, coffees and protein bars don't sustain me for a full day's work so I've learned that it's worth investing the time to prepare and pack food to take with me rather than constantly heading to a drive-through and finishing the day totally un-nourished and sluggish.

Even when I'm travelling, I will always try to make the time to eat my food undistracted – it really does make a difference, not only in how you feel, but it sets the tone for the rest of your working day. (Plus, there are no crumbs, empty packets or crushed cans floating about the car, underneath your seat, tucked in the top drawer or wedged under your keyboard.)

Small, insulated lunch bags with different compartments are widely available and are great for keeping things cool – I throw in one or two small ice-packs if I'm taking things that need to be kept chilled for more than a few hours. Thermal food containers are your best friend for keeping liquid foods warm or cold, from tea, coffee and smoothies to soups, curries and stews. Pack oatcakes, rice cakes, bread, etc. separately at room temperature, and cooked rice, quinoa, pasta or veggies chilled, so that when it's time to eat, you can simply mix through and enjoy. Foolproof foods for the road which require no temperature regulation include nuts and seeds, biltong, tinned tuna and oatcakes, fruit such as apples and bananas and recipes such as savoury muffins, pages 132–4.

Cutlery

Avoid single-use plastic cutlery; instead invest in stainless steel travel cutlery sets that come with their own case. Travel-friendly cutlery, bento boxes and flasks make great gifts for those people always on the go.

eating mindfully

Mindfulness is not a new concept, but it is one that is growing in popularity. As an umbrella term, mindfulness is a practice stemming from Zen Buddhism that encourages conscious awareness of the present moment. Mindful practices encourage people to live more intentionally and develop the skills necessary to manage modern-day living, which often revolves around the mindless consumption of news, food and social media alongside our busier yet, ironically, more sedentary lifestyle. Mindful practices have been proven to benefit us both physically and mentally, reducing depression, sleeping problems and anxiety to name a few. More recently, there's been a huge increase in research about 'mindful eating' and its potential role in addressing problematic eating behaviours, from continuing to eat beyond fullness and emotional eating to recognised disorders.

Mindful eating is the practice of becoming more mindful of not only what we eat but how we eat. I was introduced to it in Bali on a silent retreat (cliché, I know) and originally rolled my eyes, which is the reaction I have to most things that have changed my life in a positive way. I would often claim I didn't have time to sit down to eat a meal and when I did, it would usually be while hunched over a laptop or phone – sometimes both at the same time. Mindful eating is 'eating without distraction' (including smartphones, televisions, desktops or even reading) and there are many practical exercises you can try, such as becoming aware of hunger cues and using a number scale to understand them to simply making an effort to slow down and chew your food more. When I first began, I realised how disconnected I was from my body and hunger cues, eating 'because it's breakfast time' rather than because I was truly hungry, or ignoring those cues 'because I only ate a few hours ago' when I truly was hungry. It was a disheartening, difficult practice at first but consistency and a gentle persistence prevailed. The University of Berkeley found that with a mindful approach people often ate less in volume and frequency (reducing over-eating and snacking), savoured eating more and selected healthier foods.

I am far from perfect but these seemingly insignificant improvements in my eating habits and relationship with food have led to massive changes in not only what I eat but how I eat and how I feel. Calling myself out on my own BS and challenging my behaviours is uncomfortable and frustrating, but creating space around mealtimes has been important for me. Others may think it's weird to 'do nothing' whilst eating, which is funny, given that so many people are paying more attention to what's on their screens than what's on their plate or the person(s) they're with. Some of my closest friends run their entire work lives online, via email, websites, apps and social media. Whenever we hang out there's an unwritten rule that I love: that phones go away when the food comes out – not face down on the table, away. Disconnect to reconnect. Instagram will still be there when everyone's finished their ice cream.

essential staples

dips, dressings and butter coins

'Happiness is homemade'

These can transform bland ingredients such as boiled or steamed vegetables in an instant, or spice up and put new twists on salads – without relying on lots of new or perishable ingredients! Shop-bought dips and dressings are convenient to pick up and most fridges have a dedicated shelf for them (usually keeping them well past their use-by date!) But reaching for the same sauces and drowning every salad in the same dressing gets very bland, very quickly. Homemade dips, dressings and butter coins are a brilliant addition to your 'cooking toolbox' to add lots of flavour and variation to your favourite staples. Quick, easy, cheaper and arguably more delicious, you can tweak recipes depending on your own tastes and preferences. (Like more garlic in your hummus? Add more. Prefer a chunky-textured guacamole to a smooth one? Blend it less.) You'll also be using much higher-quality ingredients than the supermarket alternatives, which are usually packed with preservatives, colourings and flavourings to prolong shelf life and cut manufacturing costs.

Makes 1 X 300ML jar

OK, life-changing might be pushing it but if I could only have one recipe as an 'extra' in my fridge, this tomato and chilli relish would be it! Sweet and spicy, I use it on everything from cheese and crackers to burgers and sandwiches or spread under eggs on toast.

Life-changing tomato and chilli relish VE GF

1 tbsp olive oil
1 yellow onion, finely diced
1 garlic clove, finely chopped or grated
1 red chilli, deseeded and finely diced
4 medium tomatoes, finely diced
4 tbsp red wine vinegar
120g soft dark brown sugar
Salt and freshly ground black pepper

1. Heat the olive oil in a heavy-based saucepan over a medium heat, add the onion and garlic and stir for a minute or two until they begin to soften. Add the chilli and stir for another minute.

2. Add the tomatoes, red wine vinegar and sugar and a good pinch of salt. Bring to the boil then reduce the heat and simmer for about 1 hour, or until it's reduced to a jammy consistency. Taste and season as necessary.

3. While the relish is still warm, spoon into a sterilised jar and seal tightly. Store unopened in a cool, dark place; once opened, keep in the fridge for up to a year. Try it with the Best ever bacon and egg roll on page 53.

Serves 3–4 as a starter or side

Beautiful and bright, this dip really stands out both visually and flavourfully, injecting colour and variety in a grazing board.

Spiced beetroot dip Ⓥ ⒼⒻ

250g vacuum-packed beetroot, roughly chopped
½ tsp ground cumin
½ tsp ground coriander
½ tsp ground cinnamon
Juice of ½ lemon
Pinch of salt and pepper
3 tbsp natural yoghurt
30g shelled pistachios, roughly chopped

1. Put the beetroot into a small food processor with the spices and lemon juice and blitz until smooth. Season with a pinch of salt and pepper.

2. Spoon into a bowl and serve with the natural yoghurt swirled through and the chopped pistachios scattered over the top. Try it with the Baked falafel bites (see page 95) or Moroccan spiced lamb bites (see page 110).

Serves 5–6 as a
starter or side

Simple and easy, this spicy but cooling Mexican dip is the perfect pairing for loaded nachos, fajitas (see page 113) or even smeared on to a sandwich instead of butter.

Guacamole VE GF

2 large avocados
1 red onion, diced
1 fresh jalapeño pepper, diced
Juice of 2 limes, plus wedges to serve
Pinch of sea salt
Pinch of ground cumin
Handful of chopped coriander

1. Put everything into a small food processor and blitz together, or use a bowl and mash with the back of a fork, keeping a chunky texture.

2. Serve with another pinch of cumin, chopped coriander and wedges of lime. Try it with Slow-cooker pulled barbecue chicken sliders (see page 109) or Pineapple, chilli and lime beef fajitas (see page 113).

Serves 3–4 as a starter or side

The classic Middle Eastern dip, this is my base recipe for hummus. It's thick and creamy and goes with just about anything. Use more or less garlic, spices and lemon to make it your own.

Hummus

4 tbsp tahini
Juice of 1 lemon
4 tbsp olive oil, plus extra for drizzling
2 garlic cloves, finely chopped or grated
Pinch of salt
½ tsp ground cumin
400g tin chickpeas, drained and rinsed
Pinch of sumac, to serve
1 tbsp chopped parsley, to serve

1. In a small food processor, whizz the tahini and lemon juice first for a minute or two, scraping down the sides as you go.

2. Add the olive oil, garlic, salt and cumin and blitz again until smooth. Finally, add the drained chickpeas and blitz for 2–3 minutes.

3. Add 2 tablespoons of cold water (or more, depending on texture preference) to thin out the hummus a little. Taste and adjust as necessary with more salt, cumin or lemon juice.

4. Serve with another drizzle of olive oil, a pinch of sumac and the parsley. Try it with the Baked falafel bites (see page 95) or Moroccan spiced lamb bites (see page 110).

Each recipe makes about 8 servings (tablespoons) of dressing

Behind every good salad is a great dressing – brilliant at pulling ingredients together and adding loads of flavour. I use a small, clean jam jar and throw all the ingredients in before screwing the lid on and giving it a good shake. Old miniature jam jars make perfect lunch-box-friendly individual portions.

Dressings

Simple lemon tahini

4 tbsp tahini
Juice of 1 lemon
1 tbsp maple syrup
1 garlic clove, finely chopped or grated
2 tbsp water, to thin
Pinch of salt and pepper

Simple balsamic

4 tbsp olive oil
3 tbsp balsamic vinegar
1 tbsp honey
1 garlic clove, finely chopped or grated
Pinch of salt and pepper

Miso maple

3 tbsp olive oil
1 tbsp rice vinegar
1 tbsp maple syrup
½ tbsp soy sauce
2 tsp white miso paste

Sesame ginger

2 tbsp olive oil
2 tbsp toasted sesame oil
2 tbsp soy sauce
1 tbsp honey
1 tbsp rice vinegar
1 garlic clove, finely chopped or grated
2 tsp grated fresh ginger

Chilli lime

Zest and juice of 1 lime
2 tbsp apple cider vinegar
½ tbsp soy sauce
1 tbsp honey
3 tbsp olive oil
1 garlic clove, finely chopped or grated
Pinch of ground cumin
Pinch of chilli flakes
Pinch of salt

Honey wholegrain mustard

4 tbsp olive oil
2 tbsp apple cider vinegar
1 tbsp wholegrain mustard
1 tbsp honey
1 garlic clove, finely chopped or grated
Pinch of salt and pepper

1. Whisk your dressing ingredients together in a small bowl with a fork (or shake together in a jar with a tight-fitting lid). Taste and adjust the seasoning as necessary.

2. Store in an airtight jar in the fridge for up to 5 days.

Each recipe
makes 12 coins
(24 servings)

Both my fridge and my freezer will always have at least one sweet and one savoury variety of butter coins: throw-everything-in recipes that are incredibly versatile. I use savoury coins on everything from steamed veggies to steak or spread on toast under eggs, and sweet ones on top of pancakes, toast or warm grilled fruit. They add so much flavour to simple dishes and they also make great gifts: wrap them up like a cracker and bring along to barbecues or brunches. Food makes an excellent gift and you might even inspire somebody else to get in the kitchen too!

Savoury butter coins

Lemon and parsley

200g salted butter, softened
Large bunch of parsley, leaves and stems
   finely chopped
2 garlic cloves, finely chopped or grated
Zest of 2 lemons
2 tsp good-quality flaked sea salt

Jalapeño and lime

200g salted butter, softened
1 fresh jalapeño pepper, deseeded and
   finely chopped
Zest of 1 lime, plus a squeeze of juice
1 garlic clove, finely chopped or grated
Small handful of coriander leaves and
   stems, finely chopped
2 tsp good-quality flaked sea salt

Sundried tomato, Parmesan and basil **V** **GF**

200g salted butter, softened
50g Parmesan cheese, finely grated
Handful of basil leaves, chopped
50g sundried tomatoes in oil, drained
1 garlic clove, finely chopped or grated
2 tsp good-quality flaked sea salt

1. Combine the softened butter in a bowl with the ingredients for your chosen butter coin and mix together with the back of a fork until combined.

2. Tip the flavoured butter on to a sheet of baking paper and roll up tightly into a log, then twist the ends up like a Christmas cracker. Chill in the fridge for at least 2 hours before using.

3. Once chilled, unwrap and slice into 1cm coins (or keep the log whole to gift or slice later). If not using immediately, the wrapped log will keep in the fridge for up to 1 week or the freezer for up to 3 months.

Each recipe
makes 12 coins
(24 servings)

Sweet butter coins can be used in savoury dishes too! The Maple, brown sugar and cinnamon butter coin (made without the vanilla) and the Orange zest and honey are great on steamed carrots, green beans and other vegetables. For a Christmas version, I'll add mixed spice and cranberries and use them as gifts too.

Sweet butter coins

Maple, brown sugar and cinnamon

200g salted butter, softened
2 tbsp maple syrup
1 tbsp soft light brown sugar
½ tsp ground cinnamon
½ tsp vanilla bean paste (or use vanilla extract)
1 tsp good-quality flaked sea salt

Honeycomb

200g salted butter, softened
4 x 40g Crunchie bars (use a sharp knife to slice off the chocolate coating and chop the honeycomb into small chunks)
2 tbsp honey
1 tsp good-quality flaked sea salt

Orange zest and honey

200g salted butter, softened
Zest of 1 large orange
2 tbsp honey
Pinch of ground cinnamon
1 tsp good-quality flaked sea salt

Salted tahini and honey

200g salted butter, softened
4 tbsp tahini
4 tbsp honey
1 tsp good-quality flaked sea salt

1. Combine the softened butter in a bowl with the ingredients for your chosen butter coin and mix together with the back of a fork until well combined.

2. Tip the flavoured butter on to a sheet of baking paper and roll up tightly into a log, then twist the ends up like a Christmas cracker. Chill in the fridge for at least 2 hours before using.

3. Once chilled, unwrap and slice into 1cm coins (or keep the log whole to gift or slice later). If not using immediately, the wrapped log will keep in the fridge for up to 1 week or the freezer for up to 3 months.

breakfasts

But first, coffee

Sweet, savoury, two-before-twelve or none at all? Your first meal of the day should be a completely individual choice based on how you feel, how much time you have, your preferences and what's in (or not in) the fridge! I'd much rather enjoy freshly baked granola with cold milk in the evening and something savoury in the morning – and I don't think twice about ordering a large side of vegetables if I'm out for breakfast. That being said, if I want pancakes, I want the real deal. This chapter is made up of dishes that would fit in dotted among breakfast and brunch menus alike, but by all means – break the rules!

Serves 2

Dukkah is an Egyptian spice blend made from toasted nuts, seeds and spices; it's an incredibly easy way to add texture and flavour to simple dishes. I like to make a large jar and sprinkle it on everything from soups to avocado on toast. Here, I've used it to crust soft-boiled eggs, which makes a simple dish both look and taste amazing!

Dukkah-crusted soft-boiled eggs with charred asparagus Ⓥ ⒼⒻ ⒹⒻ

3 eggs
1 tbsp olive oil
10 asparagus spears, woody ends snapped off and sliced in half lengthways
2 spring onions, sliced on the diagonal
Handful of chopped herbs, such as parsley and dill
Lemon wedges, to serve

FOR THE DUKKAH
50g hazelnuts
50g pistachios
25g black/white or mixed sesame seeds
4 tbsp coriander seeds
2 tbsp cumin seeds
1 tbsp dried thyme
½ tsp salt
Pinch of chilli flakes (optional)
Freshly ground black pepper

1. Preheat the oven to 200°C/180°C fan.

2. First make the dukkah. Spread all the nuts on a baking tray and roast in the oven for 8–10 minutes. Meanwhile, toast all the seeds in a dry frying pan over a medium heat until toasted and fragrant.

3. Remove the nuts from the oven and while hot, rub the hazelnuts with a tea towel to remove the skins. Add the seeds, nuts and remaining dukkah ingredients to a food processor and pulse to a rough crumb; set aside.

4. Bring a saucepan of water to a gentle boil. Carefully lower in the eggs and set a timer for 6½ minutes.

5. Meanwhile, place a griddle pan or non-stick frying pan over a high heat. Add the olive oil and sauté the asparagus for 2 minutes, followed by the spring onions for another 2 minutes until both are nicely charred.

6. When the eggs are ready, remove the pan from the heat and run under cold water until the eggs are cool enough to handle. Peel the eggs over kitchen paper to absorb excess water, then roll in the dukkah crumb. (The leftover dukkah can be stored in an airtight container at room temperature for up to 3 months.)

7. Arrange the charred asparagus and spring onions on 2 plates. Slice the crumbed eggs in half and place on top of the greens. Scatter with the fresh herbs and serve with a lemon wedge, a pinch of salt and a crack of fresh black pepper.

Serves 4

Gone are the days of thin, rubbery pancakes from a pre-made protein pancake mix, drowning in zero-calorie sweetener! Creamy ricotta gives a magical custard-like texture and taste and when combined with whipped egg whites it creates velvety soft, cloudlike pancakes. Lemon zest gives them a light and tangy flavour and I like to top them with whatever seasonal fruits I have and a butter coin (see pages 34–5) or a good glug of maple syrup. If I have friends over for breakfast on the weekends, this is my go-to crowd-pleaser.

Fluffy lemon ricotta pancakes Ⓥ

220g plain flour
100g sugar
1 tsp baking powder
Pinch of salt
360ml milk
250g ricotta
4 eggs, separated
1 tsp vanilla bean paste (or use vanilla extract)
Zest and juice of 1 lemon
Butter, for frying

NOTES

· Cooked pancakes will keep in the fridge for up to 3 days, or the freezer for up to 3 months. To reheat, warm in a microwave or simply pop straight in the toaster until crisp.

· Swap the lemon zest for orange zest or add 2 tablespoons of poppy seeds to the batter.

1. Set your oven on the lowest setting and line a large baking tray with baking paper. This can be used to keep the pancakes warm while you're cooking them.

2. In a large bowl, mix the flour, sugar, baking powder and salt together. In a separate bowl, whisk together the milk, ricotta, egg yolks, vanilla, lemon zest and juice until mostly smooth (don't worry if there are some clumps from the ricotta). Pour this into the dry ingredients bowl and mix until just combined.

3. In a clean bowl, use an electric whisk to beat the egg whites until stiff peaks form, then gently fold these into the ricotta mix.

4. Place a large non-stick frying pan over a low-medium heat and lightly brush the pan with butter. Working in batches, use about 4 tablespoons of batter per pancake and cook for 2–3 minutes on each side until golden. Transfer each cooked pancake to the oven to keep warm until you are ready to serve.

Makes 1 large jar
(25 x 30g servings)

Granola is one of my favourite cupboard staples! Shop-bought versions tend to be overpriced with only a dusting of the good ingredients that I love. It's such an easy way to use up any leftover nuts and seeds and tailor each batch to whatever you fancy. Throw everything together in a bowl and then into the oven – done! I like this one served cold with yoghurt and fresh fruit or with warmed milk poured over, so the milk turns chocolatey and any chocolate drops begin to melt. For breakfast or for dessert, anything goes.

Sea salt chocolate granola Ⓥ

350g rolled oats
100g flaked almonds
100g pecans
80g coconut flakes
40g chia seeds
4 tbsp soft light brown sugar
40g cocoa powder
2 tsp sea salt
6 tbsp olive oil
6 tbsp maple syrup
2 tsp vanilla bean paste (or use
   vanilla extract)
140g dark chocolate chips or
   chunks

NOTE
· To make this vegan, use vegan chocolate; for a gluten-free version use gluten-free oats.

1. Preheat the oven to 200°C/180°C fan and line two baking trays with baking paper.

2. In a large bowl, mix together the oats, nuts, coconut flakes, chia seeds, brown sugar, cocoa powder and salt.

3. In a small pan over a low heat, warm the olive oil, maple syrup and vanilla together until just warm and then pour over the dry ingredients, mixing everything together well.

4. Spread the mixture evenly out on to the baking sheets and bake for 20–25 minutes, stirring halfway through, until toasted and golden.

5. Add the chocolate chips once the granola has completely cooled (or while it's still warm if you want them to melt). Store in an airtight container for up to 6 months.

Serves 4

The forever student in me is a sucker for tinned baked beans on toast, but these really are far more wholesome and flavourful. I make a large batch and then freeze them in portions, ready to defrost overnight. They're great piled on top of toast or baked potatoes and make a great filling in toasties, burritos or quesadillas.

Smoky chorizo beans on garlic-rubbed sourdough **DF**

1 tbsp olive oil
2 shallots, diced
60g chorizo, diced
1 garlic clove, finely chopped or grated
2 sprigs of fresh thyme, leaves stripped
1 tsp smoked paprika
400g tin cannellini beans, drained and rinsed
400g tin chopped tomatoes
2 tbsp maple syrup
4 thick slices of sourdough
2 garlic cloves, cut in half lengthways
Salt and freshly ground black pepper
Handful of chopped parsley, to garnish

NOTES
· This freezes really well. Store for up to 3 months.

· Remove the chorizo for a vegan option.

1. Place a heavy-based saucepan over a medium heat, add the olive oil and sauté the shallots until soft. Add the chorizo, garlic, thyme leaves and paprika and sauté until the chorizo begins to crisp up.

2. Pour in the cannellini beans, chopped tomatoes, maple syrup and a good pinch of salt. Bring to the boil and then reduce to a simmer for about 10 minutes to thicken. Taste for seasoning, remove from the heat and then use either a hand-held blender or a masher to partially mash the beans. Set aside while you toast the sourdough.

3. Once the bread is toasted and while still warm, rub the sliced garlic all over the sourdough slices. Pile on the smoky chorizo beans and finish with freshly cracked black pepper and chopped parsley.

Serves 2

Simple, quick and absolutely delicious. A shallot adds a touch of sweetness, the goat's cheese adds a creamy finish and using fresh herbs really does make a big difference.

Garlic and thyme mushrooms with goat's cheese on toast Ⓥ

2 tbsp butter
1 shallot, finely chopped
3 sprigs of fresh thyme, leaves
   stripped
200g mixed mushrooms (Swiss
   brown, portobello, oyster,
   shiitake), sliced
2 thick slices of sourdough
3 garlic cloves, finely chopped or
   grated
50g soft or marinated goat's
   cheese
Salt and freshly ground black
   pepper
Fresh herbs, such as parsley or
   tarragon, to serve

NOTE
· Swap the butter for olive oil and
  skip the goat's cheese to make this
  a vegan option.

1. Melt the butter in a frying pan over a medium-high heat until it begins to foam.

2. Add the shallot and fry until soft, then stir in the thyme and sliced mushrooms and cook until the mushrooms are softened. At this stage, toast the sourdough slices.

3. Add the garlic with a generous grind of salt and pepper and sauté until the toast is ready.

4. Smear the goat's cheese over the toasted sourdough and pile the mushrooms on top. Finish with a handful of freshly chopped herbs.

Serves 2

A cooling and refreshing alternative to warm porridge oats. Quinoa has a nutty flavour and is high in 'complete' (containing all nine essential amino acids) plant-based protein, as well as being full of fibre and naturally gluten-free. This is great to make ahead if you need something to grab-and-go from the fridge.

Overnight mango, coconut and lime quinoa porridge Ⓥ ⒼⒻ ⒹⒻ

120g quinoa flakes
360ml coconut milk
2 tbsp maple syrup, plus extra to serve
Zest and juice of ½ lime
1 tsp ground cinnamon
1 tsp vanilla bean paste (or use vanilla extract)
Pinch of salt
1 tbsp black sesame seeds
1 tbsp sunflower seeds
1 tbsp toasted coconut flakes
1 fresh mango, cubed
Fresh mint leaves, to garnish

1. In a bowl, combine the quinoa flakes with the coconut milk, maple syrup, lime zest, cinnamon, vanilla and pinch of salt. Divide between individual serving jars and leave in the fridge overnight.

2. Mix the sesame seeds, sunflower seeds and toasted coconut flakes together and set aside until ready to serve.

3. Serve each portion of porridge topped with fresh mango chunks, lime juice, the seed mix, fresh mint leaves and an extra splash of maple syrup.

NOTES

· The quinoa base can be stored in the fridge for up to 4 days.

· If you don't have quinoa flakes, this is a great dish to use up leftover cooked quinoa – it can be enjoyed straight away with no need to soak overnight! For 2 people, replace the quinoa flakes with 180g cooked and cooled quinoa in step 1 and use half the amount of coconut milk. Enjoy cooled or warmed in a microwave before adding your toppings.

Serves 2

Stuffed-'n'-sealed breakfast burritos were a staple starter to the day when I spent a few weeks road-tripping the west coast of America. 'Sealing' them in the final step is an absolute game changer!

Breakfast burritos

60g chorizo, diced
½ yellow onion, diced
3 eggs, beaten
2 large tortilla wraps
40g smoked Cheddar cheese, grated
Freshly ground black pepper

FOR THE SALSA
1 medium avocado, cubed
1 large tomato, deseeded and diced
1 garlic, finely chopped or grated
1 small jalapeño pepper, finely diced
Juice of 1 lime
½ tsp salt
Small handful of coriander, finely chopped

1. Make the salsa first by combining all the ingredients in a small bowl; set aside.

2. Fry the chorizo in a frying pan over a medium-high heat until it begins to release its oil, then add the diced onion and sauté until the onion is soft and the chorizo is starting to crisp. Tip onto a large plate, set aside and return the pan with any residue oil to the heat.

3. Turn the heat down to low and pour in the beaten eggs, gently folding them by pulling them from the outside into the centre with a spatula. Remove from the heat just before they set. Tip the eggs on to the plate next to the chorizo and wipe the pan clean with kitchen paper.

4. Place the pan over a high heat while you assemble the burritos: add a tortilla and layer in the fillings, starting with the scrambled eggs, then top with the chorizo and onion mix, cheese and finally the salsa and some black pepper. Wrap each tortilla by folding the sides in first followed by the top and bottom so they're tightly wrapped with no filling leaking out.

5. Once wrapped, seal the burritos by placing them in the preheated pan, seam-side down. Cook for about 30 seconds on each side until slightly toasted and golden.

NOTE
· For a vegetarian option, replace the chorizo with 60g sliced mushrooms.

Serves 4

Baked potatoes for breakfast? Sounds bizarre but not only is it an amazing way to use up leftovers but sweet potatoes also count towards the World Health Organization's '5 a day' recommendation. Sweet or savoury, pretty much anything that you'd have on toast goes! Here are some of my favourite combinations.

Breakfast baked sweet potato: two ways

4 medium sweet potatoes, scrubbed

SWEET TOPPINGS
2 tbsp coconut yoghurt, 1 tbsp almond butter, 1 sliced banana, pinch of ground cinnamon (VE)
OR
2 tbsp hazelnut butter, 30g raspberries, 2 tsp maple syrup (VE)

SAVOURY TOPPINGS
½ thinly sliced avocado, 25g crumbled feta, pinch of chilli flakes, fresh coriander (V)
OR
Leftover Smoky chorizo beans (see page 43)
OR
Leftover Garlic and thyme mushrooms (VE, see page 45)

1. Preheat the oven to 240°C/220°C fan and line a baking tray with foil.

2. Prick the potatoes all over with a fork (this allows steam to escape during baking). Bake in the oven for about 45 minutes, or until tender, turning them halfway through cooking.

3. Remove the sweet potatoes from the oven and slice open lengthways with a sharp knife. Let them cool slightly while you prepare your toppings.

NOTE
· Bake extra and keep them in the fridge for up to 5 days.

Serves 2

Forget avocado on toast, this is where it's at! Freezing-cold winter swims wouldn't be the same in Bondi if they weren't finished off with a 'Good Times Roll' sarnie – wrapped up in towels, with hot coffee and good conversation. This is my twist on their epic breakfast roll. Classic tomato sauce is great, but I always have a jar of my special tomato and chilli relish (see page 24) floating around my fridge. If I could only have it on one thing ever again, this would be it!

Best ever bacon and egg roll with paprika aioli **DF**

2 brioche buns
2 rashers of smoked bacon
2 eggs
Tomato sauce (or homemade tomato and chilli relish, see page 24)
Handful of rocket
Freshly ground black pepper

FOR THE PAPRIKA AIOLI
4 tbsp mayonnaise
½ tsp smoked paprika
Juice of ½ lemon
1 garlic clove, finely chopped or grated

1. Preheat a grill to high and line a baking tray with foil.

2. Make the paprika aioli by mixing everything together in a small bowl.

3. Place the bacon on the baking tray and grill for 8–10 minutes until crispy, turning halfway through cooking.

4. Meanwhile, place a non-stick frying pan over a high heat with a thin smear of butter or oil. Crack in the eggs, one at a time, and fry until the whites are set, about 3 minutes.

5. Cut the brioche buns in half and toast cut-side up under the grill for a minute until lightly golden.

6. To assemble, spread tomato sauce or relish on the bottom of each brioche bun, top with the bacon, egg and fresh rocket. Spread a heaped tablespoon of the paprika aioli on the brioche lid and add a crack of black pepper. Sandwich together and enjoy!

NOTE
· This is also incredible with grilled halloumi instead of bacon for a vegetarian version.

mains

'No good story started
with a (shit) salad'

say no to shit salads

Assembling a not-shit salad is not so much an art as it is an equation of layering salty, sweet, creamy, crunchy and acidic together. Textures and colours play as big a part as flavours too. There's nothing worse than a damp, limp or soggy salad, and if you're not eating it straight away or if you're making extra to last throughout the week, how you prepare and pack your salad really does make – or break – even the best of them. I really wanted salads to be a stand-alone chapter in this book as they often carry the stereotype of being 'bland' or 'boring', which is so far from the truth! I've added in lots of tips and tricks to help save time and waste and to make sure you get the best from your salads: which ones are great to make in bulk, how to refresh sad-looking salad leaves and how to keep fresh herbs *actually* fresh for over a week.

As always, I encourage you to stray from the recipes – the great thing about salads is that they're so interchangeable. Swap between protein sources – such as chicken, fish, tofu – and play around with different leaves, grains, nuts, seeds and, of course, the dressing – the most important part in my opinion! Check out pages 30–1 for more dressing combinations and say no to shit salads.

fresh is best

HOW TO PACK A NOT-SHIT SALAD

The key here, is layering. When it comes to packing your salad, make the heaviest, most sturdy ingredients (grains, beans, pasta, lentils, root vegetables) the bottom layer, with the lighter components layered on top. Leaves such as lettuce, spinach, rocket and herbs should always be near the very top. Store salad dressings either at the bottom of the jar (see the Beetroot, feta and wild rice salad on page 63) so that you can shake-and-go when ready to eat, or store the dressing separately. I like to wash out and keep any small jars (miniature jam jars are great) to use for single-serve salad dressings as they can easily fit into a packed lunchbox.

KEEPING SALAD BAGS FRESH

I try to shop for fresh foods 'little and often' but there is nothing more frustrating than buying a bag of salad only to return to it a day or two later and find lifeless, wilted leaves or a slimy ball of what was once spinach. This hack keeps leaves fresh for up to (and sometimes well over!) a week. Once you've bought your salad, remove the leaves from the bag and store them in a large food container (glass or BPA-free plastic) or a sealed ziplock bag on top of a piece of dry kitchen paper. This helps to absorb any moisture, keeping the leaves crisp and fresh. Storing them in containers also prevents them from getting crushed, bruised and bashed by heavier vegetables in the fridge. Remember, you can always wash, dry and reuse ziplock bags.

Most green leaves (spinach, lettuce, rocket) that are starting to look a bit sad can be revived by getting rid of any browned or damaged leaves and then submerging in ice-cold water for 20 minutes. This will rehydrate them and keep them fresh and crisp. Leave to air-dry and enjoy immediately.

HERBS

Herbs are an incredible way to finish dishes and add lots of colour and flavour to everything from scrambled eggs to salads – even desserts. However, they are easily one of the most wasted foods, which puts people off buying them. The best option is to grow your own but for people (like me) for whom that's not always possible, correctly storing them can preserve herbs for 2–4 weeks (really!).

Herbs fall into two categories: soft and hard. Soft herbs (parsley, coriander, dill, basil, oregano, tarragon, mint) have flexible stems and soft leaves. Store these herbs like a bouquet of flowers – snip off the very base of the stems, place in a glass jar with an inch of water at the bottom and keep in the fridge, replacing the water every few days. Basil and mint are the exceptions here as they like to be kept at room temperature, in a light room but out of direct sunlight. I buy potted-plant versions and water them regularly, removing dead leaves every few days and they last for weeks.

Hard herbs (sage, rosemary, thyme) have firm leaves and woody stems. Store these in small bunches by rolling up inside damp and wrung-out kitchen paper and then putting in a ziplock bag with a few holes pierced in it (or reuse a takeaway container and pierce a few holes in the lid).

You can also avoid wasting leftover herbs by chopping them up and using them in butter coins (see pages 32–3), or freezing in ice-cube trays in olive oil (for cooking) or water (for drinks). Once frozen, pop out the cubes and keep in a ziplock bag or storage container in the freezer.

Serves 2

Mango and avocado are the perfect summer combination and the chilli lime dressing adds a zesty kick. This is a really refreshing salad and works well with flaked salmon or halloumi too.

Grilled chicken, mango and avocado salad with cashews and chilli lime dressing GF DF

2 skinless chicken breasts
1 tbsp olive oil
2 garlic cloves, finely chopped or grated
Pinch of chilli powder or cayenne pepper
Pinch of salt
Large handful of soft leafy greens, such as lamb's lettuce and baby spinach
1 mango, peeled, stoned and sliced
1 avocado, peeled, stoned and sliced
Handful of basil, roughly torn
30g cashews, roughly chopped
Lime wedges, to serve

FOR THE DRESSING
2 tbsp olive oil
Zest and juice of ½ lime
½ tbsp apple cider vinegar
½ tbsp honey
Pinch of chilli flakes
Pinch of salt

1. Preheat the grill to high and line a baking tray with foil.

2. In a mug or small jar, whisk the dressing ingredients together with a fork.

3. Butterfly the chicken breasts in half lengthways and use your hands to rub the olive oil over each one. Place on the baking tray and sprinkle over the garlic, chilli powder or cayenne pepper and salt, gently rubbing the seasoning on to both sides of the breast. Grill the chicken for 4–5 minutes on each side, turning halfway, until golden brown.

4. Meanwhile, assemble the salad leaves and top with the mango, avocado and basil.

5. Once the chicken is cooked, thinly slice into strips and add to the salad along with the cashews. Drizzle over the dressing and serve with lime wedges.

NOTE
· This salad is best enjoyed fresh but you can cook the chicken and make the dressing in advance and keep in separate airtight containers in the fridge for up to 3 days, just add the fresh fruits and assemble when you're ready to enjoy.

Serves 2

This is one of the first salads I created to take to work in a large Mason jar. The height of the jar (as opposed to your standard rectangular lunchbox) means you can keep components separate, and by pouring the dressing in first, you keep the salad leaves from getting soggy, while the homemade kitchen paper divider keeps the nuts crunchy and fresh.

Beetroot, feta and wild rice salad with honey balsamic dressing Ⓥ Ⓖ🅕

15g pumpkin seeds
15g walnuts, roughly chopped
250g packet of ready-cooked long-grain and wild rice
½ red onion, finely diced
25g raisins or cranberries, roughly chopped
2 large handfuls of rocket
125g vacuum-packed cooked beetroot, cut into wedges
60g feta

FOR THE DRESSING
1½ tbsp olive oil
½ tbsp balsamic vinegar
½ tbsp honey
Pinch of ground cumin
Pinch of salt and freshly ground black pepper

1. In a small dry frying pan over a high heat, toast the pumpkin seeds and walnuts for 2 minutes until just coloured.

2. Whisk the dressing ingredients together with a fork or shake in a jar with a tight-fitting lid until combined.

3. In a bowl, mix the cooked rice with the red onion and raisins or cranberries.

4. If you are serving immediately, arrange the rocket on a plate and top with the rice mix and beetroot wedges. Crumble over the feta, sprinkle over the toasted nuts and seeds, then pour over the dressing.

NOTES

· Make ahead and store in an airtight container for up to 3 days but keep the dressing separate and pour over just before serving.

· To make this a salad in a jar, pour the dressing into the bottom of a large Mason jar, followed by the rice mix, beetroot wedges, feta and a large handful of rocket. Create a separate basket for the nuts by folding up a piece of kitchen paper towel to layer on top of the rocket. This will keep them crunchy!

· For another gluten-free option, you could make this using quinoa instead of rice.

Serves 2

I first had a seared tuna steak watching the sun set in Ibiza. Meaty, melt-in-your-mouth and so easy to make at home, I've paired it here with a simple and refreshing cucumber and avocado salad and a sweet and salty dressing. A really impressive-looking salad that's ready in a flash.

Seared tuna steak with cucumber and avocado salad and honey soy dressing ⓓⒻ

2 x 200g sustainably caught tuna steaks
1 medium cucumber
Handful of soft and sweet salad leaves, such as pea shoots
½ avocado, pitted, peeled and diced
Few strips of sushi ginger, thinly sliced
1 tbsp olive oil
Juice of ½ lemon
Pinch of salt
1 tbsp sesame seeds
Lime wedges, to serve

FOR THE DRESSING
1 tbsp rice vinegar
1 tbsp toasted sesame oil
½ tbsp soy sauce
½ tbsp honey
1 garlic clove
Juice of ½ lime
Pinch of chilli flakes

NOTES
· This salad is best served fresh.

· To make this gluten free use tamari in the dressing instead of soy sauce.

1. Remove the tuna steaks from the fridge about 30 minutes before cooking.

2. Whisk the dressing ingredients together with a fork and leave to one side while you prepare the salad.

3. Run a fork lengthways down the cucumber to give a ribbed texture to the skin. Slice in half lengthways (you can scoop out the watery centre with a teaspoon if you like) and then cut into thin semicircles. Place in a bowl with the salad leaves, avocado and sushi ginger.

4. Place a non-stick frying pan or griddle pan over a high heat.

5. In a small bowl, combine the olive oil, lemon juice and salt. Pat the tuna steaks dry with kitchen paper to remove any excess moisture and then rub the olive oil and lemon mixture all over the tuna steaks.

6. Place the oiled tuna steaks into the hot frying pan and cook for 60–90 seconds on each side. Once you've placed them in the pan, don't move them until you flip them over; you want them to have a nice crust on the outside but still be pink in the middle. Once seared, remove from the pan and set aside while you finish the salad.

7. Pour the dressing over the salad and gently toss it together until everything is mixed. Divide between 2 plates and sprinkle over the sesame seeds. Serve the tuna steak on the side with lime wedges.

Serves 2

This vibrant Mexican salad, which can be thrown together in under 20 minutes, is great as a stand-alone dish or as a side. If I'm going to a barbecue, I'll make a large bowl of this salad to bring along – it goes with pretty much anything!

Mexican salad bowl with crispy tortillas and lime dressing VE

2 flour tortillas
Olive oil, for brushing and frying
Pinch of cayenne pepper
200g tin sweetcorn, drained
1 baby gem lettuce, shredded
400g tin black beans, drained and rinsed
½ red onion, diced
100g cherry tomatoes, quartered
Handful of coriander, chopped
1 avocado, diced
Lime wedges, to serve

FOR THE DRESSING
2 tbsp olive oil
1 tbsp finely chopped coriander
1 tsp maple syrup
1 garlic clove, finely chopped or grated
Juice of 1 lime
Pinch of ground coriander
Pinch of salt and freshly ground black pepper

1. Preheat the oven to 220°C/200°C fan and line a baking tray with non-stick baking paper.

2. Lightly spray or brush the tortillas with olive oil, sprinkle with a pinch of cayenne and salt and cut into triangles with scissors. Arrange in one layer in the baking tray and bake for 8–10 minutes until golden and crisp.

3. Heat ½ tablespoon of olive oil in a non-stick frying pan over a medium heat, add the sweetcorn and cook for 8–10 minutes until charred and golden.

4. Meanwhile, whisk the dressing ingredients with a fork (or shake in a small jar with a tight-fitting lid).

5. In a large bowl, combine the lettuce, black beans, sweetcorn, red onion, tomatoes and coriander, then pour over the dressing and gently mix through.

6. To assemble, divide the salad mix between bowls and top with the diced avocado, lime wedges and the crispy tortilla chips.

NOTES
· Make ahead and store in an airtight container for up to 3 days, keeping the tortilla crisps separate.

· This is another great salad jar recipe; simply pour the dressing in first and layer the beans, sweetcorn, tomatoes and red onion on top, followed by a handful of shredded lettuce and the avocado. Use a folded piece of kitchen paper on top to act as a barrier between the crunchy tortilla crisps.

Serves 2

Candied nuts and seeds are so quick and easy to make – I'll often make a large batch and use them to add a sweet crunch to salads. My favourites are pecans, walnuts, sesame seeds or slivered almonds. Grilling the pear adds a smoky sweet flavour too.

Griddled pear and Parmesan salad with candied pecans and balsamic dressing Ⓥ ⒼⒻ

40g pecans, roughly chopped in half
½ tbsp butter
2 tbsp soft light brown sugar
1 pear, sliced horizontally into 5mm circles
1 tsp olive oil
140g bag of rocket
30g shaved Parmesan cheese
Salt and freshly ground black pepper

FOR THE DRESSING
2 tbsp olive oil
1 tbsp balsamic vinegar
1 tbsp honey
1 tsp Dijon mustard

1. Lay out a small sheet of baking paper for the candied pecans.

2. Toast the pecans in a dry frying pan over a high heat for 2–3 minutes until they smell nutty but before they start to brown. Remove the pan from the heat and, working quickly, add the butter and brown sugar, stirring constantly with a spatula until dissolved. Immediately pour the pecan mixture on to the baking paper, then sprinkle with a pinch of salt and leave to cool.

3. To make the dressing, whisk everything together with a fork in a mug or shake together in a small jar with a tight-fitting lid. Set aside.

4. Place a griddle pan or large non-stick saucepan over a high heat. Gently pat dry the pear slices with kitchen paper to remove any excess moisture and use your hands to very lightly brush the olive oil over them. Place the slices in the hot pan and cook for 2–3 minutes on each side until charred.

5. To assemble the salad, toss the rocket, Parmesan shavings and balsamic dressing together and divide between 2 plates. Top with the warm griddled pear and then break up the candied pecans with your hands to crumble over the top.

NOTE
· Make the candied pecans ahead and store in an airtight container for up to 2 weeks.

Serves 2

Poaching chicken is so easy and a great way to cook chicken breasts as it keeps them juicy and tender. The beautiful soft white colour looks great in salads or wraps served thinly sliced or shredded. They work wonderfully alongside a sweet and crunchy Waldorf salad; here I've used a light and tangy yoghurt dressing.

Crunchy Waldorf salad with poached chicken and honeyed yoghurt dressing GF

2 skinless chicken breasts
1 tsp salt
1 bay leaf
2 garlic cloves, smashed flat with a knife
½ lemon, sliced

FOR THE WALDORF SALAD
1 baby cos or little gem lettuce, shredded
1 celery stick, halved lengthways and very thinly sliced
1 Granny Smith apple, quartered and thinly sliced (squeeze over the juice of ½ lemon to stop them from browning)
Handful of seedless grapes, halved
40g walnuts, roughly chopped

FOR THE DRESSING
4 tbsp natural yoghurt
2 tbsp olive oil
1 tbsp honey
1 tsp Dijon mustard
Pinch of salt

1. Put all the poaching ingredients into a saucepan with enough water to cover the chicken by about 3cm and place over a medium–low heat until it reaches a very gentle simmer (bubbles barely breaking at the sides). Cook for 10–15 minutes until the chicken is cooked through. Use tongs to remove the cooked chicken and leave to cool while you prepare the salad (discard the liquid).

2. Make the dressing by whisking all the ingredients together with a fork.

3. Assemble the salad by layering the lettuce, celery, apple slices and grapes. Once the chicken has cooled, thinly slice and then add to the salad. Scatter over the walnuts and pour over the dressing.

NOTES
· Try poaching the chicken in stock or even coconut milk and add aromatics such as thyme sprigs or whole peppercorns.

· This is a great salad to make ahead – store everything in an airtight container for up to 3 days, keeping the dressing separate.

· Once cooked, poached chicken will keep for 5 days in the fridge, so it's great to make ahead and add to any other salads, wraps or sandwiches!

· To make this dairy free, use soya or coconut yoghurt in the dressing.

Serves 2

This is a simple and beautiful dish: lightly spiced cauliflower mixed with sweet raisins, crunchy flaked almonds, my favourite tahini-based dressing and as many herbs as I can get my hands on.

Roast cauliflower salad with flaked almonds, fresh herbs and tahini yoghurt dressing Ⓥ ㉓

600g cauliflower florets (1 small head)
½ tsp cumin seeds
½ tsp coriander seeds
½ tbsp turmeric
½ tsp salt
1 tbsp olive oil
100g quinoa
40g raisins
Handful each of parsley, mint and dill, chopped
30g flaked almonds
Lime wedge, for squeezing

FOR THE DRESSING
6 tbsp natural yoghurt
4 tbsp tahini
2 tsp honey
Juice of 1 lime

NOTES
· This is a really robust salad to make ahead and enjoy throughout the week. Serve as a main dish or with shredded chicken or grilled salmon.

· Store in an airtight container for up to 4 days.

· To make this vegan, use soya yoghurt and maple syrup in the dressing.

1. Preheat the oven to 240°C/220°C fan.

2. Toast the cumin and coriander seeds in a small dry frying pan over a high heat until aromatic until they begin to 'pop'. Remove from the heat and roughly crush with a pestle and mortar. Tip into a large bowl with the turmeric, salt and olive oil, toss in the cauliflower florets and mix until evenly coated in the spice mix.

3. Arrange the spiced florets on a baking tray in a single layer and roast for about 20 minutes until they are tender when pricked with a fork and beginning to char around the edges.

4. Meanwhile, cook the quinoa according to the packet instructions. Once cooked and whilst still warm fluff up with a fork and mix in the raisins and chopped parsley.

5. Toast the flaked almonds in a small dry frying pan over a medium heat until golden brown.

6. In a small bowl, whisk the dressing ingredients together with a fork.

7. To assemble the salad, smear half of the tahini yoghurt dressing on to the plates with the back of a spoon and top with the quinoa mixture and roasted cauliflower. Dollop the other half of the dressing over the top and scatter over the chopped mint and dill, toasted flaked almonds and finish with a squeeze of lime.

Serves 2

This salad is bursting with colour, crunch and a sweet and salty umami flavour from the miso dressing. A great way to use up leftover salmon fillets (from page 104), or you can buy ready-cooked salmon fillets or use good-quality tinned salmon.

Flaked salmon and Asian slaw salad with a miso maple dressing ⬤DF

2 cooked salmon fillets
Lime wedges, to serve

FOR THE SLAW
1 carrot, peeled and thinly sliced or grated
¼ small red cabbage, cored and thinly sliced
2 spring onions, thinly sliced
Handful of mangetout, thinly sliced
1 tbsp thinly sliced coriander leaves, plus extra to serve
2 tsp sesame seeds

FOR THE DRESSING
2 tbsp toasted sesame oil
1 tbsp maple syrup
2 tsp white miso paste
1 tsp soy sauce
1 garlic clove, finely chopped or grated
1cm piece of fresh ginger, peeled and finely grated
Juice of 1 lime

1. Make the dressing by whisking everything together in a mug or shaking in a small jar with a tight-fitting lid.

2. Prepare all of your vegetables and mix them together in a bowl with the dressing.

3. Divide the slaw between 2 plates and flake the salmon over the top. Serve with lime wedges, extra coriander and sesame seeds.

NOTE
· Store in an airtight container for up to 3 days.

Serves 2

Sweet potato, salty halloumi and creamy avocado combine to make a simple but delicious salad. After banana bread, this is the most popular recipe on my website.

Roasted sweet potato and halloumi salad, toasted pecans and lemon, honey and thyme dressing Ⓥ ⒼⒻ

2 sweet potatoes, cut into wedges
1 tbsp olive oil, plus extra for
   brushing
1 tsp salt
30g pecans
½ packet of halloumi (112g), cut
   into strips
2 large handfuls of salad leaves,
   such as spinach and rocket
Fresh basil
½ large avocado, sliced

FOR THE DRESSING
1 tbsp olive oil
1 tbsp honey
1 tsp fresh thyme leaves
Juice of ½ lemon
Pinch of salt

1. Preheat the oven to 240°C/220°C fan.

2. Put the sweet potato wedges in a baking tray and drizzle with the olive oil and salt. Use your hands to toss the sweet potatoes in the oil and salt, then space them out on the baking tray so they can cook evenly. Roast for about 30 minutes in the oven. Remove from the oven and allow to cool slightly.

3. To make the dressing, whisk all the ingredients in a mug with a fork or shake in a small jar with a tight-fitting lid to combine.

4. Toast the pecans over a high heat in a dry non-stick frying pan, making sure they don't burn. Set aside and wipe any crumbs from the pan, ready to fry the halloumi. Lightly brush the pan with olive oil and fry the halloumi over a high heat for 2 minutes on each side until golden and crispy.

5. To assemble the salad, mix the salad leaves and basil together and then layer on the sliced avocado, sweet potato wedges and halloumi. Crumble over the toasted pecans and pour the dressing on top.

NOTES
· Another robust salad, this will keep well for up to 4 days in the fridge.

· Store in an airtight container, keeping the dressing separate.

Serves 2

Packed full of vegetables and fibre, this is such a delicious and satisfying salad, which can be enjoyed warm or cold. I'll usually roast extra vegetables so that I can use them to top pizzas or tarts (see pages 128 and 92).

Caramelised red onion and roast fennel salad with cumin-spiced carrots, puy lentils and tahini maple dressing VE GF

2 tsp cumin seeds
2 tbsp olive oil
1 fennel bulb, halved and thinly sliced
1 red onion, halved and thinly sliced
250g Dutch or rainbow carrots, halved lengthways
250g packet of ready-cooked puy lentils
Handful of fresh herbs, such as mint, parsley and basil
Salt

FOR THE DRESSING
3 tbsp tahini
Juice of 1 lemon
1 garlic clove, finely chopped or grated
1 tbsp maple syrup
Pinch of ground cumin

NOTE
· This robust salad will keep well for up to 4 days in the fridge. Store in an airtight container, keeping the dressing separate.

1. Preheat the oven to 220°C/200°C fan.

2. Toast the cumin seeds in a small frying pan over a medium-high heat until fragrant and they 'pop'. Remove from heat and use a pestle and mortar to crush them.

3. Pour half the oil into a baking tray and add the sliced fennel and red onion and a pinch of salt. Pour the remaining oil into a separate baking tray and add the carrots, crushed cumin seeds and a pinch of salt. Toss both trays to coat everything in the oil and evenly space out the vegetables.

4. Roast the carrots for 25 minutes and the red onion and fennel for about 10 minutes longer, until the vegetables are tender when pricked with a fork and beginning to char around the edges. Meanwhile, whisk all the dressing ingredients together with a pinch of salt until well combined.

5. Warm the lentils up in a frying pan over a medium heat with a splash of water to stop them from sticking.

6. To assemble the salad, divide the lentils between 2 plates and top with the roasted vegetables. Pour over the dressing and scatter with a large handful of fresh herbs.

Serves 2

This is a great way to use up leftover meat from roasts, although if cooking from fresh it only takes a few minutes to whip up.

Steak, apple and walnut salad with wholegrain mustard dressing GF

½ tbsp olive oil
½ tbsp butter
2 good-quality fillet or sirloin steaks
1 green apple, quartered and very thinly sliced
30g dried cranberries or cherries
30g walnuts, roughly chopped
Large handful of mixed salad leaves, such as spinach or rocket

FOR THE DRESSING
2 tbsp olive oil
1 tbsp maple syrup
½ tbsp wholegrain mustard
½ tbsp apple cider vinegar
1 garlic clove, finely chopped or grated
Pinch of salt and freshly ground black pepper

1. Preheat a non-stick frying pan over a medium–high heat, then sear the steaks for 2–3 minutes on each side until bronzed on the outside but pink on the inside. Transfer to a plate to rest while you prepare the salad.

2. Prepare the dressing by whisking all the ingredients in a mug or shaking in a small jar with a tight-fitting lid.

3. Assemble the salad by tossing all the remaining ingredients together. Thinly slice the steak and add to the salad. Drizzle over the dressing and serve.

NOTES
· Store in an airtight container for up to 3 days, keeping the dressing separate.

· Use lemon juice to keep the apple slices from oxidising and turning brown.

· This combination of ingredients also works well with leftover roast turkey, chicken or grilled halloumi.

Serves 4

When there's nothing fresh in the fridge, this salad can be knocked up in under 20 minutes. Feel free to add any other cupboard essentials you might have, such as jarred olives, artichokes, roasted peppers, tinned sweetcorn or tuna. Grated Parmesan is great to keep as a frozen staple to sprinkle over this before serving.

Store-cupboard sundried tomato pasta salad VE

250g dried pasta (any shape)
200g frozen peas
10 sundried tomatoes in oil, plus
    2 tbsp oil from the jar
2 tbsp olive oil
1 tbsp apple cider vinegar
1 garlic clove
1 tsp dried oregano
Salt and freshly ground black
    pepper

1. Bring a saucepan of salted water to the boil over a high heat. Add the pasta and cook according to the packet instructions, adding the frozen peas for the last 2 minutes. Drain and run the pasta under a cold tap to cool. Leave to drain while you make the sauce.

2. In a small food processor, blend the sundried tomatoes with the oils, apple cider vinegar, garlic, oregano and a pinch of salt and pepper until smooth.

3. Combine the pasta and tomato sauce until mixed through. Taste and adjust the seasoning, then serve.

NOTE
· Store in an airtight container for up to 5 days.

vegetables

Eating more plants benefits our health. Research has proved time and time again that a diet high in fruits, legumes and vegetables is linked with a lower risk of diabetes, heart disease, strokes and obesity. The easiest way to up your vegetable intake is to experiment with new recipes, make them your own and where possible, make larger portions so that they're readily available when you need to conjure up last-minute meals. Roasted vegetables, especially red onions, baby potatoes, spiced cauliflower, sweet potatoes and other root vegetables, are always on rotation in my fridge. Simple steamed greens such as asparagus, tenderstem broccoli and green beans take less than 10 minutes to prepare and are an easy side dish to most meals. Adding a portion of vegetables in at breakfast is a great way to get more in. See pages 38–50.

Serves 4

Earthy and sweet, beetroots are one of my favourite vegetables and roasting them with balsamic vinegar adds more depth to their flavour. Serve with a swirl of yoghurt and some crunchy bread; I also like to sprinkle over some hazelnut and pistachio dukkah (see page 38). Simple yet beautiful.

Roast beetroot, balsamic and thyme soup

500g raw beetroots, scrubbed and cut into cubes
3 tbsp olive oil
2 tbsp balsamic vinegar
2 sprigs of thyme, leaves removed
1 yellow onion, sliced
2 leeks, sliced
1.5 litres vegetable stock
Sea salt and freshly ground black pepper

TO SERVE
4 tbsp natural yoghurt
4 tbsp dukkah (see page 38)
Chopped fresh dill

1. Preheat the oven to 220°C/200°C fan.

2. Place the cubed beetroot on a baking tray and drizzle over half the olive oil, the balsamic vinegar, thyme leaves and a good pinch of salt. Roast in the oven for 45–60 minutes until the beetroot is tender and starting to caramelise.

3. Meanwhile, heat the remaining olive oil in a heavy-based saucepan over a medium heat and sauté the onion and leeks until soft and translucent, about 15 minutes.

4. Stir the roasted beetroot chunks into the pan and pour over the stock. Bring to the boil then reduce to a simmer for 5 minutes. Remove from the heat and then use a hand-held blender to blitz the soup until it's smooth. Season to taste.

5. Pour into bowls and top each with a dollop of natural yoghurt, a tablespoon of dukkah, some fresh dill and a good crack of black pepper.

NOTES
· Store in the fridge for up to 5 days or freeze for up to 3 months.

· To make this dairy free, use coconut or soya yoghurt.

Serves 4

My work often requires me to spend time travelling, involving lots of time driving, plenty of overnight stays away from home and nearly every meal 'on the road'. Until in-car fridges become a thing, a good-quality thermos flask was my absolute saviour. Soups are of one the easiest go-to recipes to stash in a thermos and I have fond memories of enjoying this nourishing green soup tucked up in my car waiting for my windscreen to defrost.

Coconut, spinach and pea green soup

2 tbsp butter
2 shallots, diced
2 garlic cloves, finely chopped or grated
1 large white potato, diced
500ml vegetable stock
400ml tin coconut milk
200g frozen peas
200g spinach
Sea salt and freshly ground black pepper

TO SERVE
Lemon juice
Handful of chopped herbs, such as basil, coriander or parsley
Freshly grated nutmeg (optional)
Toasted sourdough spread with a savoury butter coin (see pages 32–3)

NOTES
· Store in the fridge for up to 5 days or freeze for up to 3 months.

· To make this dairy free, use olive oil instead of butter.

1. Melt the butter in a heavy-based saucepan over a medium heat and sauté the shallots with a pinch of salt until soft. Add the garlic, cooking for a minute or two until aromatic, then add the potato and cook for a further minute, ensuring everything is mixed together.

2. Add the stock and bring to the boil, then reduce to a simmer for about 15 minutes, or until the potato is cooked and tender when pricked with a fork.

3. Add the coconut milk, peas and spinach and simmer for another 5 minutes, allowing the spinach to wilt and the peas to cook. Use a hand-held blender to process until smooth; taste and adjust the seasoning if necessary.

4. Finish with a squeeze of lemon juice, the chopped herbs, grated nutmeg (if using) and a good crack of black pepper. Serve with toasted sourdough and a butter coin.

Serves 4

I'll always have some of this soup stashed away in my freezer for when I want something wholesome and filling without having to worry about too much washing-up or extra effort. A few oatcakes with thick slices of Cheddar to accompany this and I couldn't be more satisfied.

Spiced red lentil, tomato and butter bean soup (VE) (GF)

2 tbsp olive oil
1 yellow onion, diced
4 garlic cloves, diced
2 tsp ground cumin
2 tsp medium curry powder
Pinch of chilli flakes (optional)
400g tin chopped tomatoes
2 tbsp tomato purée
1 litre vegetable stock
2 carrots, diced
150g red split lentils, rinsed
400g tin butter beans, drained and rinsed
Lemon juice
Handful of chopped parsley
Salt and freshly ground black pepper

NOTE
· Store in the fridge for up to 5 days or freeze for up to 3 months.

1. Heat the olive oil in a heavy-based saucepan over a medium heat, add the onion and a pinch of salt and sauté for 8–10 minutes until soft and translucent.

2. Add the garlic and cook for another minute until aromatic, then add the cumin, curry powder and chilli flakes (if using). Stir everything together for a minute or two until well mixed and then pour in the chopped tomatoes, tomato purée and another pinch of salt. Cook for 5 minutes over a medium heat.

3. Pour in the stock, diced carrots, lentils and butter beans and bring everything to the boil, then reduce to a simmer and cook for about 20 minutes until the lentils are tender.

4. Use a hand-held blender to partially blend the soup, leaving a chunkier texture (or blend until completely smooth, if preferred). Taste and adjust the seasoning if necessary.

5. Serve in bowls finished with a squeeze of lemon, the parsley, some freshly cracked black pepper and an extra pinch of chilli flakes.

Serves 2

This no-frills recipe can be ready in under 20 minutes and allows the simplicity of the classic combination of tomatoes, basil and Parmesan to shine through. I'm all for buying more supermarket-brand produce but with olive oil I always buy the best quality I can find because it really does make a big difference.

Blistered tomato, olive oil and basil spaghetti ⓥ

4 tbsp olive oil, plus extra to
   serve
1 garlic clove, finely chopped
400g cherry tomatoes
Large handful of fresh basil leaves
½ tbsp balsamic vinegar
250g spaghetti (fresh or dried)
30g Parmesan cheese, finely
   grated
Salt and freshly ground black
   pepper

NOTES
· Store in the fridge for up to 3 days.

· To make this dairy free, use nutritional yeast instead of Parmesan.

1. Heat the oil in a heavy-based saucepan over a low–medium heat and add the garlic. Cook for 2 minutes until it starts to go soft and golden, being careful not to burn it.

2. Add the whole cherry tomatoes and ½ teaspoon of salt. Cook for 15 minutes until the tomatoes begin to blister and burst, releasing their juices.

3. Finely chop the basil (leaves and stalks), reserving a few whole leaves to garnish. Add the balsamic vinegar and chopped basil to the pan and turn the heat to low.

4. Meanwhile, bring a large saucepan of salted water to boil. Cook the pasta for 1 minute less than it says on the packet instructions. Drain, reserving a few tablespoons of the starchy pasta water. Add these to the simmering tomatoes and stir everything together. Taste for seasoning and adjust with more salt if necessary.

5. Plate up the pasta using tongs to swirl it gently on to the plates. Top with freshly torn basil leaves, finely grated Parmesan cheese, a small drizzle of olive oil and lots of freshly cracked black pepper.

Serves 6

The Italian vegetarian alternative to lasagne, this recipe tastes even better the next day once the flavours have developed. I often serve it as a stand-alone main dish with a fresh and simple salad on the side. Served warm, the cheese is melted, bubbling and stringy; served at room temperature the next day, the flavours are even more intense. It truly is an all-rounder dish that I adore.

Aubergine parmigiana

4 aubergines, cut lengthways into 5mm slices
3 tbsp olive oil
2 garlic cloves, finely chopped or grated
2 x 400g tins chopped tomatoes
2 tbsp tomato purée
2 tbsp maple syrup
2 tsp dried oregano
1 tbsp balsamic vinegar
150g mozzarella, grated
125g Parmesan cheese, grated
1 egg, beaten
50g breadcrumbs
Fresh basil, to garnish
Salt

NOTES
· To make ahead, wrap in cling film at the end of step 4 and keep refrigerated for up to 3 days.

· To store once cooked, leave to cool completely and keep in the fridge for up to 4 days or freeze for up to 6 months.

· To make this gluten free, use gluten-free breadcrumbs.

1. Preheat the oven to 200°C/180°C fan and line a baking tray with non-stick baking paper.

2. Lightly brush each side of the aubergine slices with 1 tablespoon of the olive oil. Lay them in a single layer on the lined baking tray and season with a little salt, then roast in the oven for about 40 minutes, turning halfway, until they are golden and tender.

3. Meanwhile, heat the remaining olive oil in a saucepan over a medium heat and fry the garlic for a minute until aromatic, then add the chopped tomatoes, tomato purée, maple syrup, oregano, balsamic vinegar and a good pinch of salt. Reduce the heat to low and simmer for 20 minutes until the aubergines are ready.

4. To assemble, lightly grease a large ovenproof dish (30 x 20cm) and spoon in a few tablespoons of the tomato sauce as a base. Next, lay a single layer of the aubergine slices packed tightly together, followed by a handful of scattered mozzarella and Parmesan, reserving a large handful of Parmesan for the top. Repeat (you should get about 3 layers).

5. Finish by pouring the beaten egg over the top and sprinkling over the breadcrumbs and remaining Parmesan. Bake for about 30 minutes until bubbling and browning. I like to slide it under a hot grill for the last 2–3 minutes so the top goes golden and crispy.

6. Remove from the oven and leave to cool a little. This is best served warm (not piping hot).

Serves 6

A lunchbox favourite, store sliced frittata on a folded piece of kitchen paper to keep it from going soggy. This is a fresh, spring recipe that can be enjoyed warm or cold with a simple side salad or steamed greens.

Asparagus, pea and new potato frittata

250g new potatoes, quartered
100g asparagus tips
150g frozen peas
1 tbsp olive oil
1 yellow onion, sliced
2 garlic cloves, finely chopped or grated
2 handfuls of spinach
8 eggs
80ml milk
80g Cheddar cheese, grated
Fresh herbs, such as parsley, mint or dill, to garnish
Salt

1. Preheat the oven to 200°C/180°C fan.

2. Put the quartered potatoes into a saucepan of cold salted water and bring to the boil. Once boiling, cook for 5 minutes until tender but still with some bite, then add the asparagus tips and peas and cook for 1 more minute. Drain and set aside.

3. Heat the olive oil in a large non-stick frying pan over a medium–low heat and add the onion. Sauté until soft, then add the garlic and spinach and cook until the spinach has wilted.

4. Whisk the eggs, milk and half of the grated cheese in a large bowl. If you're using an ovenproof frying pan – with a metal handle – pour the egg mixture over the vegetables and make sure the vegetables are evenly distributed. If not, transfer the cooked vegetables to a casserole dish and pour the egg mixture over.

5. Sprinkle over the remaining grated cheese and bake in the oven for 30–40 minutes. I like to put this under a very hot grill for the last 2–3 minutes so it gets a nice bubbly crust. Remove from the oven or grill and allow to cool before removing from the frying pan or dish and cutting into slices. Serve garnished with fresh herbs.

NOTE
· Keep in the fridge for up to 3 days.

Serves 4

Peanut butter lends creaminess to this curry, whilst ginger and Thai paste add heat, maple syrup sweetness and lime a refreshing finish. Loaded with texture, colour and flavour, this is a great Thermos flask-friendly recipe when I'm out. This light but filling dish won't leave you feeling sluggish for the afternoon.

Sweet potato, peanut butter and chickpea curry VE GF

2 tbsp olive oil
1 yellow onion, diced
2 garlic cloves, finely chopped or grated
3cm piece of fresh ginger, peeled and grated
3 tbsp red Thai curry paste
2 sweet potatoes, cut into 1cm cubes
4 tbsp peanut butter
400ml tin coconut milk
400g tin chickpeas, drained and rinsed
Juice of 1 lime
2 tbsp maple syrup
Large handful of spinach, Swiss chard, rainbow chard, kale with stalks removed or other greens
Fresh herbs, such as coriander or Thai basil
Handful of roasted peanuts, chopped, to serve
Pinch of red chilli flakes
Salt

1. Place the olive oil in a heavy-based saucepan over a medium heat. Add the onion and a pinch of salt and cook until softened and translucent. Add the garlic and ginger and cook for another minute or two, until aromatic.

2. Stir in the red Thai curry paste, then add the sweet potatoes, peanut butter and coconut milk. Fill the emptied tin up with water (400ml) and add that in too. Bring to the boil then simmer, uncovered, for 20–25 minutes until the sweet potatoes are tender when pierced with a fork

3. Add the drained chickpeas and cook for another minute or two until warmed through. Add the lime juice and maple syrup. Taste for seasoning and adjust as necessary.

4. Remove from the heat and add the spinach, leaving it to wilt (if using other, tougher greens add these in with the chickpeas).

5. Garnish with fresh herbs such as coriander or Thai basil, chopped peanuts and a pinch of red chilli flakes and serve with rice.

NOTE
· Store in the fridge for up to 5 days or in the freezer for up to 3 months.

Serves 6

Similar to a pizza, savoury tarts are an easy throw-together solution and great for using up leftovers like roasted vegetables. I used to avoid anything pre-made, such as ready-rolled puff pastry, assuming it wouldn't be 'as good' as homemade (my mum makes incredible pastry, so it's pretty hard to beat!), but when baking queen herself, Mary Berry, said she can't tell the difference and often 'cheated' to save time and mess, I was converted. Cheap to buy, convenient to store, I use all-butter pastry.

Mixed tomato, gouda and pesto tart

375g sheet of ready-rolled puff
   pastry
3 tbsp tomato purée
125g gouda, sliced
50g sundried tomatoes
2 large tomatoes, sliced
80g cherry tomatoes, quartered
1 egg, beaten
3 tbsp pesto
Fresh basil leaves, to garnish
Salt and freshly ground black
   pepper

NOTES

· This is best served fresh from the oven but it will keep in the fridge for up to 2 days. Store on folded kitchen paper to prevent the bottom from going soggy.

· Can be eaten warm or at room temperature. You can even warm it up in a microwave – the pastry will lose its crispiness but it is still delicious, making it a great lunchbox option.

1. If you are using frozen puff pastry, defrost it overnight in the fridge or at room temperature 1–2 hours before you start cooking, but don't unroll it until you're ready to use it. Preheat the oven to 220°C/200°C fan.

2. Unroll the puff pastry on to a large, flat oven tray lined with a non-stick baking sheet. Use a sharp knife to gently score a two finger-widths, border around the edge of the pastry. This will puff up into a beautiful, flaky crust.

3. Spread the tomato purée over the base of the pastry, keeping within the scored border. Top with the gouda, followed by the mixed tomatoes and season with salt and pepper.

4. Use a pastry brush or your fingers to paint the beaten egg all over the pastry border; this gives it a shiny, golden finish. Season with salt and pepper and bake for 20–25 minutes, or until the pastry is crisp and golden and the base is cooked.

5. Once baked and still warm, dot the pesto over the top and scatter with fresh basil leaves. Serve with a simple side salad such as rocket with a balsamic dressing.

Serves 4–6

Serve as a stand-alone meal with a simple side salad or as a side dish with grilled halloumi or fish. Use any leftover veggies to top pastry tarts (see page 92) or pizzas (see page 128) or stir into a frittata (see page 87). This is a super-simple and tasty recipe that has endless leftover possibilities!

Roasted vegetable traybake with garlic croutons VE

2 courgettes, cubed
1 red and 1 yellow pepper, cubed
4 garlic cloves, unpeeled
2 red onions, sliced into wedges
4 tbsp olive oil
1 tsp cumin seeds
1 tbsp dried oregano
Pinch of chilli flakes
300g cherry tomatoes on the vine
Handful of parsley leaves
2 slices of sourdough or ciabatta
   bread, sliced into rough 2cm
   cubes
40g pine nuts, toasted
Handful of basil leaves, to garnish
Salt and freshly ground black
   pepper

1. Preheat the oven to 200°C/180°C fan.

2. Mix the courgettes, peppers, garlic cloves and red onions in a large bowl with 3 tablespoons of the olive oil and the spices and oregano and season with a generous pinch of salt and pepper.

3. Spread the vegetables out in 2 large roasting tins and roast for 15 minutes. Use a fork to carefully pick out the garlic cloves and set aside to cool. Give the vegetables a good stir, add the cherry tomato vines and roast for another 10 minutes.

4. Squeeze the garlic cloves from their skins and use a fork to mash them into the remaining olive oil in a small bowl. Add a handful of torn parsley and some salt and pepper, then toss in the cubes of bread and mix together. Sprinkle this and the pine nuts over the roasting tray and roast for another 5 minutes until the croutons are crispy and all the vegetables are cooked, with the tomatoes bursting and releasing their juices.

5. Remove from the oven, give everything a good mix and serve scattered with torn basil leaves.

NOTES
· Store any leftovers in an airtight container for up to 3 days.

· To make this gluten free, use gluten-free bread.

Serves 3–4

Versatile and full of Middle-Eastern flavours and spices, I love these baked falafels stuffed into wraps or toasted pitta breads with fresh rocket or as part of a mezze grazing board with some raw veggies and hummus (see page 29).

Baked falafel bites ⓋⒺ ⒼⒻ

4 tbsp olive oil
200g dried chickpeas, soaked overnight, or for at least 4 hours
2 shallots, finely diced
4 garlic cloves, finely chopped or grated
½ tsp ground cumin
½ tsp ground coriander
½ tsp ground cinnamon
Handful of coriander leaves, chopped
Handful of parsley leaves, chopped
Sea salt and freshly ground black pepper

1. Preheat the oven to 200°C/180°C fan. Pour 2 tablespoons of the olive oil into a large, deep baking tray and put into the oven to warm while you make the falafel patties.

2. Drain the chickpeas thoroughly and then add to a food processor with the remaining olive oil, shallots, garlic, spices, chopped coriander, parsley and some salt and pepper. Blitz until smooth and combined.

3. Using damp hands, take a heaped tablespoon of the mixture and shape into a golf ball, then press down with the heel of your hand into a disc shape. Repeat until all the mixture is used up (you should get about 12 falafels).

4. Carefully remove the baking tray from the oven and arrange the falafels in a single layer. Bake for 30 minutes, turning over halfway, until golden and crispy on both sides.

NOTE
· Store any leftovers in an airtight container in the fridge for up to 5 days.

fish

The key to success is to start before you're ready

I was never a huge fan of seafood until I spent a few months living in Jersey, a beautiful, tiny island between England and France bursting with French culture, cobbled town centres and beautiful beaches. Famous for their creamy Jersey milk and Jersey royal potatoes, they have a big fresh fish market and some incredible independent foodie spots, with lots of seafood on offer.

If you're new to cooking it can be quite daunting, but studies show that those who spend even a little amount of time in the kitchen are more creative and enjoy a healthier lifestyle. James Clear, author of *Atomic Habits*, writes about the power of making small, incremental changes. High in protein and easy and quick to cook, these fish dishes are especially good during the week if you don't have much time, and are a great place to start expanding your skills in the kitchen.

Serves 2

Scallops are a simple yet impressive dish. Use a very hot, preheated pan and always pat the scallops dry to remove excess moisture – this ensures a crisp, golden crust and a juicy, buttery centre.

Seared scallops with lemon, garlic and parsley linguine

125g fresh linguini (or use 90g dried)
1 tbsp olive oil
12 scallops, corals (pink bits) removed
2 tbsp butter
2 garlic cloves, finely chopped
75ml white wine
Juice of ½ lemon, plus extra to serve
Large handful of parsley leaves, roughly chopped
Salt and freshly ground black pepper

1. Bring a large saucepan of salted water to the boil and cook the linguini according to the packet instructions.

2. Meanwhile, place a large, non-stick frying pan over a high heat – you want the pan to be piping hot to sear the scallops. Once hot, add the olive oil and allow to heat up while you gently pat the scallops dry with kitchen paper. Season both sides of each scallop with a little salt.

3. Place each scallop in the pan and leave to cook for 90 seconds–2 minutes on each side. Don't move them around the pan, apart from to flip them halfway.

4. Once both sides have been seared, remove the scallops and turn the heat down to very low. Add 1 tablespoon of the butter and, when melted, tip in the garlic and leave to cook for about a minute, just until it goes golden (you don't want it to burn).

5. Pour in the white wine to deglaze the pan and then add the lemon juice. Leave for another minute until it's reduced by about half and then melt in the last tablespoon of butter.

6. Drain the pasta, reserving 2 tablespoons of the water to add to the butter sauce. Stir this through the sauce and then add the drained linguine to the pan. Stir through the parsley, reserving a little to garnish.

7. Divide the linguini between 2 plates and top with the scallops, plenty of freshly ground black pepper, the reserved parsley and a generous squeeze of lemon juice.

Serves 4

Tender baked fish, zingy slaw, creamy avocado and a spicy sauce. Fresh, flavourful and on the table in 20 minutes. Get creative with extra toppings and build your own taco station with friends or family.

Flaky fish tacos with a honeyed lime slaw and creamy chipotle sauce

500g cod fillets (or other flaky, firm white fish, such as tilapia, halibut, mahi-mahi)
1 tbsp olive oil
8 small corn tortillas, warmed
Fresh avocado, diced

FOR THE TACO SEASONING
2 tsp smoked paprika
1 tsp chilli powder
½ tsp salt

FOR THE CREAMY CHIPOTLE SAUCE
250g Greek yoghurt
1 tbsp chipotle paste or sauce
Juice of 1 lime
Pinch of salt

FOR THE SLAW
¼ red cabbage, cored and leaves shredded
100g sweetcorn, drained
4 tbsp natural yoghurt
2 tbsp fresh coriander leaves, finely chopped
1 tbsp honey
Juice of 1 lime
Pinch of salt

TO SERVE
Fresh or jarred jalapeño chillies, sliced
Lime wedges
Hot sauce
Chopped coriander

1. Preheat the oven to 200°C/180°C fan and line a baking tray with non-stick baking paper.

2. Prepare the taco seasoning, chipotle sauce and slaw by combining all the ingredients in 3 separate bowls, then set aside.

3. Pat the cod fillets dry with kitchen paper to remove any excess moisture and then use your hands to evenly coat the fish with the taco seasoning so that all sides are covered. Place on the lined baking tray, drizzle over the olive oil and bake for 10–12 minutes, or until cooked through, opaque and easily flaked with a fork.

4. To assemble the tacos, fill a tortilla with flaked fish, diced avocado, slaw, a drizzle of the chipotle sauce and any extra toppings such as jalapeños, fresh coriander and hot sauce.

NOTES
· Keep any extras stored separately in the fridge for up to 3 days.

· To make this dairy free use coconut or soya yoghurt.

Serves 4

Nothing beats a fish finger sandwich on thick-cut white bread. In this recipe, I've used panko breadcrumbs for a crispier texture and baked them beforehand to get lots of flavour and golden colour without the need for deep frying them. Paired with a wasabi mayonnaise and zesty lime, this is an elite fish finger sandwich!

Gourmet panko-crumbed fish finger sandwich with wasabi mayo

100g panko breadcrumbs
Spray oil
40g Parmesan cheese, finely grated
2 tsp paprika, plus 1 pinch
500g cod fillets
4 tbsp plain flour
1 egg, beaten
8 slices of thick-cut white bread
Handful of fresh watercress or crunchy salad leaves
Lime wedges, for squeezing
Salt and freshly ground black pepper

FOR THE WASABI MAYO
4 tbsp mayonnaise
1 tsp wasabi paste
Juice of 1 lime
Pinch of salt

1. Preheat the oven to 220°C/200°C fan and line a baking tray with non-stick paper.

2. Spread the panko breadcrumbs out evenly on another baking tray and use a spray oil to lightly coat them, then bake for 3–4 minutes until golden. Remove from the oven and tip into a bowl with the grated Parmesan, 2 teaspoons of paprika and a pinch of salt and pepper.

3. Cut the fish into chunky strips and pat dry with kitchen paper. Set up a dipping station by placing the flour in one bowl with a pinch of paprika and some salt and pepper, the beaten egg in a second bowl and the panko crumb and Parmesan mixture in a third bowl.

4. Individually dip the strips of fish into the flour, egg and finally the panko crumbs, pushing the crumbs in with your fingertips. Place the strips of crumbed fish on to the lined baking tray and bake for 12–15 minutes until the fish is cooked through and the crumbs are golden.

5. Meanwhile, make the wasabi mayo by whisking everything together with a fork.

6. Assemble each sandwich by thinly smearing the wasabi mayo on two slices of bread and sandwiching in the warm panko fingers, crispy salad, fresh cracked black pepper and squeeze of lime.

NOTE
· Panko breadcrumbs are widely available in the worldwide or Asian food aisle. Using regular breadcrumbs will also work but result in a slightly less crispy texture.

Serves 4

A simple sweet-and-sticky marinade does all of the work here. Whether you have 20 minutes or 12 hours, it's ready in a flash and delicious served simply with rice or as part of a stir-fry.

Sticky honey soy and sesame prawns

6 tbsp honey
3 tbsp soy sauce
2 garlic cloves, finely chopped or grated
1cm piece of fresh ginger, peeled and grated
450g raw prawns (fresh or frozen and defrosted), peeled and veins removed
1 tbsp olive oil
4 spring onions, thinly sliced
1 tbsp sesame seeds
Lime wedges
Pinch of chilli flakes (optional)

1. Make the marinade by whisking the honey, soy sauce, garlic and ginger together.

2. Place the raw prawns in a bowl or ziplock bag with half of the marinade, reserving the other half for later. Marinate in the fridge for at least 20 minutes, or up to 12 hours.

3. Place a large non-stick frying pan over a high heat, add the oil and stir-fry the prawns until they're pink and cooked through. Add the other half of the marinade and stir so everything is combined.

4. Serve the prawns scattered with the spring onions, sesame seeds, lime wedges and some chilli flakes, if you like a bit of a kick. These are perfect on a bed of basmati rice to soak up the sticky marinade.

NOTE
· To make this gluten free use tamari instead of soy sauce.

Serves 4

Quick and delicious, this is my favourite way to enjoy salmon – full of flavour and buttery soft. I pair the fillets with simple boiled potatoes, a herby butter coin and some steamed green vegetables.

Crispy-skinned salmon fillets with herby new potatoes **GF**

800g baby new potatoes (or Jersey royals if you can find them!)
4 sustainably caught salmon fillets
2 tbsp olive oil
1 butter coin (see pages 32–3)
OR
2 tbsp of butter, 2 chopped garlic cloves and a handful of chopped parsley or tarragon
Salt and freshly ground black pepper

1. Put the potatoes into a large saucepan of cold water, with enough to cover them by about 3cm. Add a large pinch of salt and bring to the boil, then reduce the heat slightly and cook for 18–20 minutes until the potatoes are tender when pricked with a fork.

2. Place a non-stick frying pan over a high heat and pat the salmon fillets dry with kitchen paper, then season them with salt and pepper all over.

3. Add the olive oil to the hot pan and wait a minute until the oil is hot, before adding the salmon fillets, skin-side down (laying them away from you so you don't get splashed by hot oil). Cook for 4 minutes without moving them, then use tongs to turn the fillets over and cook for another minute or two to sear the top and each side of the salmon. Remove from the heat and leave to rest while you dress the potatoes.

4. Drain the potatoes and tip into a bowl. While they are still hot, add the butter coin (or the butter, garlic and chopped herbs). Season with salt and pepper and toss to coat.

5. Serve the salmon with the herby potatoes and some steamed seasonal vegetables.

NOTES

· I always make extra salmon and potatoes for the next day. I don't find steamed vegetables keep too well, so I'll throw together some crisp sliced sugar snap peas, cucumber and baby spinach to make a salad with a simple lemon dressing.

· Store in an airtight container in the fridge for up to 3 days.

· Buy bulk bags of salmon fillets and store in the freezer, so you can remove fillets as and when you need them.

meat

Put down your phone and pick up your life

When it comes to meat, dairy and animal products I always encourage quality over quantity. Where possible, get to know your local butcher, bakery or farm. A good butcher will be able to tell you where the meat is from and also advise you on various cuts, cooking methods and serving suggestions (from side dishes to paired wines), as well as offering a wider selection and better-quality meats, usually cut and prepared in front of you for a similar price to supermarkets (or cheaper).

However, and perhaps more importantly, I'm a firm believer in making the best with what you have. Busy households, remote locations, children, disabilities, multiple jobs, shift-work, finances and other socioeconomic factors come into play when it comes to what we buy and how we cook. I want to help make simple food special, but more importantly, help make it *accessible*. Do the best you can with what you have.

Serves 8

This is one of my favourite recipes in the whole book. It's ideal for larger groups and perfect to serve in the slow cooker surrounded by a build-your-own-burger station. And it's the gift that keeps on giving: use leftovers piled on top of nachos or pizza (see page 128), alongside slaw (see page 101), or in a grilled cheese toastie.

Slow-cooker pulled barbecue chicken sliders with chipotle lime mayonnaise

2 tbsp olive oil
8 skinless and boneless chicken thighs
2 yellow onions, halved and sliced
2 garlic cloves
2 tsp paprika
200g barbecue sauce
4 tbsp honey
2 tbsp tomato purée
1 tbsp Worcestershire sauce
2 tbsp soft light brown sugar
1 tsp salt
Juice of 1 lime

FOR THE CHIPOTLE LIME MAYONNAISE
8 tbsp mayonnaise
1 tbsp chipotle paste
1 tsp smoked paprika
Juice of 1 lime
Pinch of salt

TO SERVE
8 brioche buns
2 avocados, thinly sliced

1. Set the slow cooker to low. Warm 1 tablespoon of the olive oil in a frying pan over a medium–high heat and brown the chicken thighs in batches, transferring them to the slow cooker as you go.

2. Add the remaining oil to the pan and fry the onions until they're soft and translucent, then add the garlic and paprika and sauté for another minute, then transfer to the slow cooker.

3. Add the remaining ingredients, except the lime juice, straight into the slow cooker and cook for 6–8 hours on low.

4. Once the chicken is ready, turn off the heat and shred it with 2 forks. Squeeze over the lime juice and then leave to cool and absorb the flavours for at least 15 minutes before serving. Meanwhile make the chipotle lime mayonnaise by whisking all the ingredients together with a fork.

5. Toast the brioche buns under a hot grill. Assemble the sliders with the pulled chicken on the bottom, sliced avocado and chipotle mayo on top.

Serves 4

Sweetly spiced lamb studded with jewels of raisins in each bite, these are small but pack a lot of taste. I keep mine simple and serve them with tzatziki dip and a simple salad, or stuffed into a toasted pitta bread or wrap with crunchy butter lettuce, tzatziki and a large handful of fresh herbs.

Moroccan spiced lamb bites with easy tzatziki

500g lamb mince
1 yellow onion, finely chopped
50g panko (or normal) breadcrumbs
1 egg
2 garlic cloves, finely chopped or grated
50g raisins, roughly chopped
2 tsp ground cumin
2 tsp ground coriander
1 tsp ground cinnamon
Handful of coriander leaves, chopped
Handful of parsley leaves, chopped
2 tbsp olive oil
Sea salt and freshly ground black pepper
Mint leaves, to serve (optional)

FOR THE TZATZIKI
½ cucumber
170g Greek yoghurt
1 tbsp olive oil
1 garlic clove, finely chopped or grated
1 tbsp chopped mint leaves

1. Preheat the oven to 220°C/200°C fan and line a baking tray with non-stick baking paper.

2. To make the tzatziki, slice the cucumber in half lengthways and use a spoon to scrape out and discard the seeds. Grate or finely chop the cucumber and mix with the Greek yoghurt, olive oil, garlic and mint leaves and season with a pinch of salt and pepper.

3. For the lamb bites, put all of the ingredients, except the olive oil, into a bowl and mix well with your hands. Use a tablespoon to measure out scoops of the mixture and roll in your hands to form 18–20 roughly ping-pong-sized balls.

4. Arrange the balls on the baking paper and gently flatten into discs with the palm of your hand. Drizzle with the olive oil and bake for 20–25 minutes until browned and cooked through.

5. Serve alongside the tzatziki, scattered with mint leaves.

NOTE
· This is great to make ahead: it will keep in the fridge for up to 3 days or the freezer for 3 months.

Serves 4

An easy and colourful one-tray bake packed full of flavour with minimal washing-up. This makes enough to split up into lunches over the week.

Sticky honey and mustard one-tray chicken with Brussels sprouts and new potatoes GF DF

4 tbsp olive oil
2 tbsp honey
1 tbsp wholegrain mustard
4 garlic cloves, smashed
Juice of 1 lemon
4 skinless and boneless chicken thighs
300g Brussels sprouts, trimmed and halved
300g new potatoes, halved or quartered if large
1 red onion, cut into 8 wedges
Salt and freshly ground black pepper

1. Preheat the oven to 210°C/190°C fan.

2. In a bowl, use a fork to whisk together 2 tablespoons of the olive oil, the honey, mustard, garlic, lemon juice and a pinch of salt and pepper. Pour this marinade into a ziplock bag and place the chicken thighs inside to marinate while you prepare the vegetables.

3. Scatter the Brussels sprouts, potatoes and red onion into a large baking tray (20 x 30cm) with the remaining olive oil and a generous pinch of salt. Remove the chicken thighs from their bag and tuck snugly among the vegetables, then pour over the marinade.

4. Roast for 35–40 minutes until the chicken is golden brown, the Brussels sprouts are crispy and the potatoes are tender.

NOTE
· Store any leftovers in the fridge for up to 3 days.

Serves 6

A student staple, fajita kits were a go-to for quick group dinners. While I'm not denying there's a market for them, they can be quite dry and bland. Packet spice mixes have enzymes added to help tenderise the meat, but I've used pineapple juice, which contains an enzyme (bromelain) that does the job.

Pineapple, chilli and lime beef fajitas

750g steak (skirt, rump or flank)
1 tbsp olive oil
2 yellow onions
3 red peppers
8 fajita wraps

FOR THE MARINADE
2 tbsp olive oil
Juice of 3 limes
2 tbsp Worcestershire sauce
60ml fresh pineapple juice (100% pure is best)
2 garlic cloves, finely chopped or grated
2 tsp ground cumin
1 tsp smoked paprika
1 tsp (or less) chilli powder
1 tsp salt
Salt and freshly ground black pepper

TO SERVE
Sour cream
Salsa
Guacamole (see page 28)
Coriander leaves
Smoked Cheddar cheese

1. To make the marinade, put all of the ingredients into a bowl and whisk with a fork until combined. Add the steak and marinate for at least 30 minutes at room temperature, or in the fridge for 2–6 hours (remove from the fridge 30 minutes before cooking).

2. Preheat a cast-iron or non-stick frying pan over a high heat until really hot, add the steak to the pan and cook for 3 minutes on each side – longer if you like your steak more well done. Remove from the pan and set aside to rest for 10 minutes, loosely covered in foil, while you cook the vegetables.

3. Turn the heat down to medium and add the olive oil, onions and peppers with a good pinch of salt and cook until tender and slightly charred. Remove from the heat.

4. Warm up your wraps whilst you thinly slice the steak on an angle. Serve everything together with extra toppings and lime wedges so that everyone can build their own fajita.

NOTES
· Use any leftover steak for sandwiches, fajita salad bowls or alongside scrambled eggs for breakfast.

· Pineapple juice in cartons has often been heat-treated so the enzyme bromelain will be inactive; however, if it's all you can get your hands on, it still works in this recipe to impart flavour and sweetness.

· You can also use chicken breasts or thighs instead of steak.

Serves 2

A well-cooked fillet steak needs only a few factors: room temperature meat, a hot pan, butter to baste and add flavour and time to rest. Fillet steak is an expensive cut of meat – but following these steps will make it worth it every time.

Fillet steak with rosemary sweet potato wedges and steamed greens GF

2 fillet steaks
2 sweet potatoes, scrubbed and
    cut lengthways into 1cm wedges
3 tbsp olive oil
2 tbsp fresh rosemary leaves,
    chopped
1 tbsp butter or 1 butter coin (see
    pages 33–4), plus extra to serve
200g tenderstem broccoli
Large handful of spinach
Salt and freshly ground black
    pepper

NOTE
· Make extra sweet potato wedges to
  pack in lunchboxes throughout the
  week; they will keep in an airtight
  container in the fridge for up to
  5 days.

1. Remove the steaks from the fridge 30 minutes before you want to cook them and preheat the oven to 220°C/200°C fan.

2. Toss the sweet potato wedges into a bowl with 1½ tablespoons of the olive oil, the rosemary and a generous pinch of salt and lay in a single layer in a large roasting tin. Roast for 25–30 minutes, turning halfway, until tender and golden.

3. Place a cast-iron or non-stick frying pan over a high heat until hot, add the remaining oil to the pan and pat the steaks with kitchen paper to remove excess moisture. Season the steaks generously on both sides with salt and pepper, pressing the seasoning into the meat.

4. Use tongs to place the steaks in the pan (it should be sizzling hot) and cook for 2–3 minutes before flipping (once the steaks are in the pan, don't move them, so you get a really nice charred crust). Cook for 2 minutes on the other side, then add the butter or butter coin and baste this all over the meat. Use tongs to 'seal' the edges of the steak, then remove from the pan and transfer to a plate, pouring the pan juices over. Leave to rest, loosely covered in foil, for 10 minutes.

5. Steam the broccoli for 4–5 minutes until tender, adding the spinach for the last minute until it just wilts.

6. Serve the steak with the sweet potato fries, greens and a knob of butter (or use a small butter coin).

Serves 4

The famous Borough Market, in London, used to have a posh-dog stand with queues reaching all round the market, rain or shine. Good-quality sausages piled high with fresh, sweet and salty toppings. You can, of course, use vegetarian sausages here too.

Gourmet hotdogs: two ways

4 good-quality sausages
4 brioche sausage buns

FOR THE THAI CHILLI PEANUT HOTDOGS
1 carrot, cut lengthways into thin
   ribbons
½ cucumber, cut lengthways into
   thin ribbons
4 tbsp crunchy peanut butter
1 tbsp sweet chilli sauce
½ tbsp sesame oil
½ tbsp soy sauce
½ tbsp honey
Juice of 1 lime
2 spring onions, finely chopped
Large handful of coriander leaves
Pinch of chilli flakes

FOR THE CARAMELISED ONION, MELTED
   GRUYÈRE AND THYME HOTDOGS
1 tbsp butter
1 tbsp olive oil
2 red onions, thinly sliced
1 tbsp soft light brown sugar
1 tbsp wholegrain mustard
40g Gruyère cheese, grated
2 sprigs of thyme, leaves stripped
Pickled jalapeños, to garnish
Freshly ground black pepper

For the Thai chilli peanut hotdogs

1. Peel the carrot and cucumber then place on kitchen paper to absorb any excess water.

2. In a small bowl, use a fork to whisk together the peanut butter, sweet chilli sauce, sesame oil, soy sauce, honey and lime juice to make a sauce.

3. Grill, barbecue or roast the sausages according to the packet instructions. Slice the buns lengthways, two-thirds through, open and lightly toast.

4. To assemble, put a sausage in a bun and top with cucumber and carrot ribbons, chopped spring onions, peanut sauce, fresh coriander and chilli flakes.

For the caramelised onion, melted Gruyère and thyme hotdogs

1. Heat the butter and olive oil in a frying pan over a low–medium heat, then add the onions. Fry for 20 minutes until very soft. Turn the heat up to high, stir through the sugar and mustard and cook until caramelised.

2. Meanwhile, cook the sausages and slice the brioche lengthways, two-thirds through, open and lightly toast.

3. To assemble, put a sausage in a bun and top with the onions and Gruyère. Place under the grill on a foil-lined baking tray for 1–2 minutes until the cheese is melted.

4. Remove from the grill, sprinkle with thyme and jalapeños and season with pepper.

Serves 4

Chicken satay skewers remind me of wandering through the food stalls in Pai, a small laid-back town in north Thailand, with a much slower-paced, hippie-vibe way of life than the full-moon parties of Koh Phangan. Food has such a unique way of connecting us with memories and this dish, cooked over hot coals and served on a banana leaf after a long day of exploring, hostel-hopping and backpacking, brings back some of my favourites.

Marinated chicken satay skewers with peanut dipping sauce **DF**

500g skinless chicken breasts or
   thighs, cut into cubes
8 bamboo skewers
1 tbsp olive oil
Chopped peanuts, to garnish
Lime wedges, to serve

FOR THE MARINADE
50ml tinned coconut milk
1 tbsp curry powder
1 tsp soft light brown sugar
1 tsp red Thai curry paste
Pinch of salt

FOR THE PEANUT DIPPING SAUCE
4 tbsp smooth peanut butter
1 tbsp soft light brown sugar
1 tbsp dark soy sauce
½ tbsp red Thai curry paste
150ml tinned coconut milk
Juice of 1 lime

1. Make the marinade by mixing everything in a bowl until combined. Add the chicken, tossing until it's coated. Cover and marinate in the fridge for at least 1 hour, or overnight.

2. Soak your bamboo skewers in water for at least 30 minutes before using to stop them from burning.

3. To make the peanut sauce, put everything into a saucepan over a low heat and stir to combine, adding a few extra tablespoons of coconut milk if needed to get the desired consistency. Taste and adjust the seasoning with more lime juice or soy sauce.

4. Place a large non-stick frying pan over a medium heat and add the olive oil. Thread roughly 4 chunks of marinated chicken on to each skewer and fry in batches for about 2–3 minutes each side until cooked through and golden.

5. Serve sprinkled with chopped peanuts, the dipping sauce and lime wedges on the side.

NOTE
· To make this gluten free, use tamari instead of soy sauce.

Makes 4 large
stuffed patties

Using a smoked Cheddar, such as Applewood, gives this juicy burger a deep, smoky flavour with the kick of jalapeño. You don't need to worry about lots of toppings because there's so much flavour stuffed in the burgers; I like mine with sour cream, Guacamole (see page 28) and a cold beer.

Smoked Cheddar and jalapeño stuffed beef burgers

4 tbsp cream cheese
60g smoked Cheddar cheese, grated
1 tsp garlic powder
1 fresh jalapeño pepper, deseeded and diced
800g beef mince
1 garlic clove, finely chopped or grated
2 shallots, finely chopped
Salt and freshly ground black pepper
Olive oil, for brushing

TO SERVE
Crusty white ciabatta burger buns
Sour cream
Guacamole (see page 28)

1. In a small bowl, mix the cream cheese, grated Cheddar, garlic powder and jalapeño pepper until well combined.

2. In a large bowl, mix the beef mince with the garlic and shallots. Season well with salt and pepper. Divide the mince into 4 equal portions, then halve each single portion and flatten out into 2 patties. Scoop a heaped tablespoon of the cream cheese mixture on to the centre of one of the patties and place the other one on top. Use your hands to mould the patties together, making sure the cream cheese centre is well hidden inside. Repeat for the remaining patties then chill the burgers for at least 20 minutes, or until ready to cook.

3. Preheat the grill to high or place a griddle pan over a medium–high heat. Lightly brush the burgers with olive oil and then place under the grill or into the hot griddle pan and cook for 6–7 minutes each side until the juices run clear.

4. Slice the burger buns in half and and toast under the grill or sliced-side down in the hot pan to mop up any burger juices. Spread sour cream on the bottom of each bun, top with a stuffed burger patty, a dollop of guacamole and the top half of the bun.

NOTE
· These are best eaten fresh but uncooked burger patties can be frozen for up to 3 months.

Serves 2

Smoky and sweet, this is the perfect spring or summer pasta dish. Make twice as much and keep some for lunch tomorrow.

Pea, burrata and pancetta tagliatelle

60g pancetta
1 tbsp olive oil
1 shallot, diced
1 garlic clove, finely chopped or grated
½ red chilli, deseeded and finely sliced (or pinch of chilli flakes)
200g frozen peas
125g fresh tagliatelle (or use 90g dried)
Handful of chopped parsley
40g burrata (or mozzarella), torn
1 tbsp grated Parmesan cheese
Salt and freshly ground black pepper
Torn mint and basil leaves, to garnish
Lemon wedges, to serve

1. Bring a large saucepan of water to the boil with a pinch of salt.

2. Meanwhile, sauté the pancetta in a dry frying pan over a medium–high heat for about 5 minutes until it starts to crisp up. Add the oil and the shallot and sauté for another 5 minutes until soft, then add the garlic and chilli and stir through for a minute or two until aromatic.

3. Add the frozen peas, turn the heat down to low and cover the pan with a lid while you cook the pasta. Add the tagliatelle to the pan of boiling water and cook for 1 minute less than the packet instructions. Drain, reserving about ½ mug (125ml) of the pasta water.

4. Tip the pasta back into the pan with the reserved pasta water, then add in the pancetta, shallots and peas, add the chopped parsley and mix everything together. Season to taste.

5. Divide between 2 plates and top with torn burrata. Finish with the grated Parmesan, a few mint and basil leaves, some freshly ground black pepper and serve with the lemon wedges.

NOTE
· Store in an airtight container in the fridge for up to 2 days.

Serves 8

I had this dish at dinner one winter night in Sydney, wrapped up with a glass of red wine – and I've been obsessed with it ever since! It requires minimal effort as the slow cooker does all the work and the lamb is buttery soft after 8 hours of simmering. Leftover ragu makes a great shepherd's pie base or jacket potato topping.

Slow-cooked lamb ragu with pappardelle pasta

4 tbsp olive oil
1.2kg boneless lamb shoulder, cut into 3–4 chunks
1 yellow onion, finely diced
2 carrots, finely diced
3 celery sticks, finely diced
4 garlic cloves, finely chopped or grated
2 tbsp tomato purée
375 ml (½ bottle) red wine
250ml beef stock
400g tin chopped tomatoes
6–8 sprigs of fresh rosemary, tied with twine (optional, but easier to remove)
125g fresh pappardelle pasta (or use 90g dried)
Salt and freshly ground black pepper
Fresh basil and shaved Parmesan cheese, to serve

NOTE
· Store in an airtight container in the fridge for up to 3 days or in the freezer for up to 3 months.

1. Set your slow cooker to low and heat 2 tablespoons of the olive oil in a deep, heavy-based saucepan over a high heat.

2. Use kitchen paper to pat the lamb dry of excess moisture, then season with salt. In batches, if necessary, seal the lamb for 2–3 minutes on each side until browned all over, then transfer to the slow cooker.

3. Using the same saucepan, lower the heat to medium and add the remaining oil. Sauté the onion, carrots and celery with a good pinch of salt for about 10 minutes until softened and beginning to caramelise. Add the garlic and tomato purée and cook for 2 minutes.

4. Deglaze the pan by pouring in the wine and simmering over a medium heat until reduced by half. Transfer to the slow cooker over the lamb, then add the stock and chopped tomatoes, along with the rosemary.

5. Cook on low for about 8 hours. The meat should fall apart very easily. Turn off, shred the meat with 2 forks and leave to absorb the flavours for at least 15 minutes while you cook the pasta. Season to taste.

6. Bring a large saucepan of salted water to the boil and cook the pasta for 1 minute less than recommended on the packet. Drain, reserving about 4 tablespoons of the water for each dish you'll be serving.

7. Return the pasta to the pan with the reserved water, then mix in the lamb and sauce. Serve with basil, Parmesan and black pepper.

in betweens (and afters)

get baked

Raisin cookies that look like chocolate chip cookies are the main reason I have trust issues

My first introduction to the kitchen came through baking. Driven by a sweet tooth and an unexplained gravitational pull towards the baking aisle, I started with the safe option of shop-bought packet mixes for friends' birthday cakes at university, slowly graduating to making recipes from scratch, before eventually creating recipes myself. More than just a form of creativity, baking (especially when it's done for others) comes with a host of psychological benefits. Moreover, I think that when you start to learn and understand ingredients and become more aware of what goes into your food, whether homemade or shop-bought, it can, in turn, make you more conscious (and grateful) about what you're consuming. Baking specifically has been shown to be helpful for people who have difficulty expressing their feelings in words to show thanks, appreciation or sympathy. My response to friends' achievements is usually along the lines of 'sounds like an excuse to bake to me'.

Makes 8 x 18cm
pizzas

Homemade pizza is a great way to get started in the kitchen and this dough is very forgiving, plus you can get creative with your favourite toppings. There's real satisfaction in bringing together a handful of ingredients, and it tastes better than any shop-bought pizza. Use a pizza oven, or turn up your oven as high as it will go.

Homemade pizza ⓥ

7g active dried yeast
330ml warm water
500g strong white bread flour,
    plus extra for dusting
2 tsp salt
2 tbsp olive oil
40g polenta, for dusting

TOPPING SUGGESTIONS (PER PIZZA)
2 tbsp tomato purée
25g grated cheese, such as
    Cheddar or Gruyère
Leftover roasted vegetables, such
    as red onion and butternut
    squash
Pinch of sea salt
Handful of fresh rocket
Drizzle of olive oil
Handful of torn basil leaves

1. Activate the yeast by sprinkling it into a jug of 'bath-water-warm' water. Leave for 5 minutes until foaming.

2. Mix the flour, salt and oil in a large bowl. Pour in the yeast water and use a spoon to form a wet dough.

3. Knead the dough on a lightly floured surface for 8–10 minutes until you have a firm and smooth ball. It will still be quite sticky but shouldn't stick to your hands. Put in a lightly oiled bowl and cover with cling film. Leave to rise in a warm place for 1 hour, or until doubled in size.

4. Uncover and punch the dough firmly once to remove air pockets. Tip onto a floured surface and cut into 8.

5. Preheat the oven to 240°C/220°C fan (or the highest setting) and put two large flat baking trays inside.

6. Roll one portion of dough into an 18cm circle on a lightly floured surface. Scatter some polenta over a sheet of baking paper and transfer the dough to it. Add the toppings, then remove the tray from the oven and gently pull the paper to slide the pizza onto the tray. Scatter over a pinch of salt and cook for 10–12 minutes until the cheese is bubbling and the crust is golden.

7. Once cooked, scatter with rocket, a drizzle of oil and basil. Repeat with the remaining pizza bases.

NOTES
· Wrap dough portions in cling film and store in a ziplock bag in the fridge for up to 1 week or the freezer for up to 1 month. Bring to room temp for 30 minutes before rolling.

· If you have a stand mixer, use the dough hook to mix and knead the dough.

Makes 1 large
focaccia

This is one of my favourite dipping breads for soup but it's equally good as a starter, served with good-quality olive oil and balsamic vinegar; the flavours seep into the holes and pockets of the bread.

Garlic and rosemary focaccia Ⓥ

280ml warm water
2 tsp honey
7g active dried yeast
500g strong white bread flour
9 tbsp olive oil, plus extra for
   greasing and drizzling
1 tbsp flaked sea salt, plus extra
   for sprinkling
4 tbsp fresh rosemary leaves
   (stripped from 8 sprigs)
4 garlic cloves, finely chopped or
   grated

1. Mix the honey into the warm water in a jug and then sprinkle the yeast over the water. Leave for 5 minutes until it's foamy.

2. Put the flour, 6 tablespoons of the olive oil and the tablespoon of salt into a large bowl and mix together, then pour in the yeast water and use a spoon to bring everything together into a dough.

3. Use your hands to knead for 8–10 minutes on a lightly floured surface until the dough is smooth and elastic. It should still feel soft but shouldn't stick to your hands.

4. Lightly grease a large clean bowl with olive oil and place the dough in it, rolling it around to coat in olive oil, then cover with cling film and leave in a warm spot to rise for 1 hour, or until the dough has doubled in size. Meanwhile, generously oil a deep 20 x 30cm baking tray.

5. When the dough has risen, remove the cling film and punch the dough firmly once to release any air bubbles. Tip the dough into the oiled baking pan and stretch and flatten it to fit. Use your fingers to firmly press all over the dough creating the focaccia dimples, pressing right down to the base of the pan.

6. Mix the remaining oil with the rosemary leaves and garlic and then pour this all over the top of the focaccia. Cover again with a warm, damp tea towel and leave to prove for about 45 minutes.

7. Preheat the oven to 240°C/220°C fan and once proved, sprinkle the focaccia generously with sea salt and bake in the oven for 20–22 minutes until the top is lightly browned.

8. Remove from the oven and 'feed' the dough by drizzling over a little more olive oil. Serve whilst still warm.

NOTES

· To make this vegan, use sugar instead of honey.

· If you have a stand mixer, use the dough hook attachment to mix and knead the dough.

Makes 8
large muffins

Packed full of flavour, savoury muffins make the perfect lunchbox addition. They don't need to be refrigerated to stay fresh and you don't need any cutlery to eat them. If I have early morning flights, I'll always stash one of these in my hand luggage.

Butternut squash, spinach and feta muffins ⓥ

Spray oil (optional)
4 tbsp olive oil, plus extra for greasing
380g butternut squash, cubed
240g plain flour
1 tsp baking powder
½ tsp bicarbonate of soda
¼ tsp freshly grated nutmeg
120ml buttermilk
1 tsp Dijon mustard
2 large eggs
2 handfuls of spinach, chopped
60g Cheddar cheese, grated
60g feta, crumbled
Salt and freshly ground black pepper

1. Preheat the oven to 210°C/190°C fan and place 8 muffin liners into a muffin tin. Lightly spray the inside of each muffin liner with spray oil or run your finger around them with some olive oil.

2. Put the butternut squash, 2 tablespoons of the olive oil and a pinch of salt into a baking tray and toss to evenly cover. Roast in the oven for 20 minutes until tender.

3. Put the flour, baking powder, bicarbonate of soda, nutmeg and ½ teaspoon of salt into a large bowl and mix together.

4. In a measuring jug, mix together the buttermilk, remaining 2 tablespoons of olive oil, mustard, eggs and some freshly ground black pepper until combined.

5. Pour the wet mixture into the dry ingredients and mix together until just combined. Gently fold in three-quarters of the cooked butternut squash, spinach, Cheddar and half the feta.

6. Spoon the mixture into the muffin liners (they should be quite full), then press the remaining butternut squash and crumbled feta on top. Bake for about 20 minutes until golden. I like to put these under a hot grill for another 1–2 minutes so the tops of the muffins crisp up and brown.

NOTE
· Store in an airtight container at room temperature for up to 4 days.

Makes 8
large muffins

These flavour combinations were created using ingredients that I pretty much always have in my kitchen. Play around with your favourite ingredients and combinations, and throw in any leftover odds and ends from the fridge to create your own.

Sundried tomato, pesto and Parmesan muffins ⓥ

Spray oil (optional)
2 tbsp olive oil, plus extra for
   greasing
240g plain flour
1 tsp baking powder
½ tsp bicarbonate of soda
½ tsp salt
120ml buttermilk
1 tsp balsamic vinegar
2 tbsp pesto
2 large eggs
4 spring onions, chopped
100g sundried tomatoes, chopped
80g grated Cheddar cheese
40g grated Parmesan cheese
Freshly ground black pepper

1. Preheat the oven to 210°C/190°C fan and place 8 muffin liners into a muffin tin. Lightly spray the inside of each muffin liner with spray oil or run your finger around them with some olive oil.

2. Put the flour, baking powder, bicarbonate of soda and salt together in a large bowl.

3. In a measuring jug, mix the buttermilk, olive oil, balsamic vinegar, pesto, eggs and some black pepper together until combined.

4. Pour the wet mixture into the dry ingredients and mix together until just combined. Gently fold in the spring onions, sundried tomatoes, grated Cheddar and half the Parmesan.

5. Spoon the mixture into the muffin liners (they should be quite full), then scatter over the remaining Parmesan. Bake for about 20 minutes until golden. I like to put these under a hot grill for another 1–2 minutes so the tops of the muffins crisp up and brown.

NOTE
· Store in an airtight container at room temperature for up to 4 days.

Makes 12 cupcakes

I use coffee to enhance the flavour of the cocoa here. It's optional, but it makes a huge difference; if you don't like coffee, I promise you can't taste it. Buttermilk and oil keep the sponge light and fluffy, as chocolate bakes can be a bit dry. Topped with salted caramel and an extra pinch of flaky sea salt, these are something special.

Chocolate cupcakes with salted caramel buttercream icing Ⓥ

105g plain flour
20g cocoa powder
½ tsp baking powder
½ tsp bicarbonate of soda
75g soft light brown sugar
75g caster sugar
½ tsp salt
60ml light olive oil
90ml buttermilk
1 large egg
½ tsp vanilla bean paste (or use vanilla extract)
1 tsp instant coffee mixed into 90ml boiling water

FOR THE BUTTERCREAM
200g unsalted butter, at room temperature
500g icing sugar
50g dulce de leche or salted caramel sauce, plus extra for drizzling

1. Preheat the oven to 180°C/160°C fan and line a cupcake tray with 12 paper cupcake cases.

2. Sift the flour, cocoa, baking powder and bicarbonate of soda into a large bowl. Add both sugars and the salt and mix with a wooden spoon until well combined.

3. Add the oil, buttermilk, egg and vanilla, mixing to a thick batter. Pour in the coffee and mix again – the batter will be quite runny, but this is what we are looking for!

4. Pour the mixture into the paper cases, filling them about half-full. I pour my batter into a measuring jug with a lip first so I have a little more control over pouring. Bake for 18–20 minutes, or until a metal skewer or toothpick comes out clean when inserted into the centre. Remove from the oven and cool completely before icing.

5. Using a hand-held electric whisk, combine the buttercream ingredients until evenly mixed and smooth. Add a few tablespoons of milk to loosen, if needed, until it's the consistency of toothpaste.

6. Spoon or pipe the buttercream on to the cupcakes and top with a drizzle of warmed caramel sauce.

NOTES
· The cupcakes can be made ahead, cooled and stored (un-iced) in an airtight container for up to 3 days or frozen for 3 months.

· Buttercream can be stored separately in an airtight container for 2 weeks in the fridge or 3 months in the freezer.

Makes 8 (using
90ml lolly moulds)

As well as being a great way to introduce children into the kitchen, making your own ice lollies is fun, easy and requires no oven! Adapt the ingredients to whatever flavours you fancy and experiment; when they're ready, enjoy them 'naked' or take them to the next level, drizzled or dunked in chocolate and crunchy toppings.

Coconut and coffee lollies with dark chocolate and a Biscoff crumb ⓥ

400ml tin coconut milk
6 tbsp maple syrup
1 tsp vanilla bean paste (or use
   vanilla extract)
Pinch of salt
250ml strong black coffee, cooled
100g dark chocolate
4 Biscoff biscuits

NOTES

· I prefer using silicone moulds. To unmould, I fill a sink with a few inches of warm water and submerge the lolly tray for bursts of 10 seconds until it's easy to wiggle the lollies out of the moulds.

· Keep 'naked' lollies in the freezer, stored in ziplock bags, for up to 3 months.

· To make these vegan, use vegan chocolate.

1. In a NutriBullet or blender, blend the coconut milk, maple syrup, vanilla and salt together.

2. Slowly pour about 3 tablespoons of the coconut mixture into each mould, then pour in the coffee, dividing equally between the moulds. Top each one with the remaining coconut mixture. This will give an 'ombre' effect.

3. Add the lids and popsicle sticks and put into the freezer for at least 5 hours or overnight.

4. Once frozen, remove the moulds from the freezer and lay out on a sheet of baking paper while you make the topping.

5. Put the Biscoff biscuits into a ziplock bag and use a rolling pin to gently crush them. Put three-quarters of the chocolate in a heatproof bowl set over a saucepan of just simmering water (making sure the bottom of the bowl doesn't touch the water). When melted, remove from the heat and add the remaining chocolate, stirring until everything has melted together.

6. Remove the lollies from their moulds and either individually dunk the top half of each lolly in the chocolate for a hard chocolate shell, or lay all of the lollies down on the baking paper and drizzle the chocolate over. Finish with a sprinkle of the Biscoff crumb before the chocolate completely sets.

Makes 6 (using
90ml lolly moulds)

Coconut and lime lollies with dark chocolate and toasted coconut ⒼⒻ

400ml tin coconut milk
Zest and juice of 1 lime
4 tbsp maple syrup
Pinch of salt
100g dark chocolate
2 tbsp toasted desiccated coconut

NOTES

· I prefer using silicone moulds. To unmould, I fill a sink with a few inches of warm water and submerge the lolly tray for bursts of 10 seconds until it's easy to wiggle the lollies out of the moulds.

· Keep 'naked' lollies in the freezer, stored in ziplock bags, for up to 3 months.

· To make these vegan, use vegan chocolate.

1. In a NutriBullet or blender, blend the coconut milk, lime zest and juice together with the maple syrup and salt.

2. Pour the mixture into 6 lolly moulds, add the lids and popsicle sticks and put in the freezer for at least 5 hours or overnight.

3. Once frozen, remove from the freezer and lay out on a sheet of baking paper while you make the topping.

4. Put three-quarters of the chocolate in a heatproof bowl set over a saucepan of just simmering water (making sure the bottom of the bowl doesn't touch the water). When melted, remove from the heat and add the remaining chocolate, stirring until everything has melted together.

5. Remove the lollies from their moulds and either individually dunk the top half of each one in the chocolate for a hard chocolate shell, or lay all of them down on the baking paper and drizzle the chocolate over. Finish with a sprinkle of toasted desiccated coconut before the chocolate completely sets.

Peanut butter, banana and yoghurt lollipops with milk chocolate and roasted peanuts Ⓥ ⒼⒻ

250g natural or Greek yoghurt
2 bananas, chopped
140g smooth peanut butter
4 tbsp maple syrup
1 tsp vanilla bean paste (or use vanilla extract)
Pinch of salt
100g milk chocolate
30g salted roasted peanuts, roughly chopped

1. In a NutriBullet or blender, blend the yoghurt, bananas, peanut butter, maple syrup, vanilla and salt together.

2. Slowly pour into the moulds and add the lids and popsicle sticks. Freeze for at least 5 hours or overnight.

3. Once frozen, remove from the freezer and lay out on a sheet of baking paper while you make the topping.

4. Put three-quarters of the chocolate in a heatproof bowl set over a saucepan of just simmering water (making sure the bottom of the bowl doesn't touch the water). When melted, remove from the heat and add the remaining chocolate, stirring until everything has melted together.

5. Remove the lollies from their moulds and either individually dunk the top half of each lolly in the chocolate for a hard chocolate shell, or lay all of them down on the baking paper and drizzle over the melted chocolate. Finish with a sprinkle of roasted peanuts before the chocolate completely sets.

NOTES

· I prefer using silicone moulds. To unmould, I fill a sink with a few inches of warm water and submerge the lolly tray for bursts of 10 seconds until it's easy to wiggle the lollies out of the moulds.

· Keep 'naked' lollies in the freezer, stored in ziplock bags, for up to 3 months.

Serves 12

Putting the 'ease' in cheesecake, this is a great recipe to get the kids involved. If I'm making this for an occasion, I like to make it the day before I plan to serve it, so that I don't have to worry about being in the kitchen on the day. Creamy, velvety and rich – perfect for effortless entertaining.

White chocolate, ginger and lime no-bake cheesecake Ⓥ

250g digestive biscuits, crushed
120g butter, melted
6 balls of stem ginger, finely chopped
Pinch of salt
250ml double cream
300g full-fat cream cheese, softened
100g white chocolate, melted and slightly cooled
4 tbsp stem ginger syrup
Zest and juice of 2 limes
Grated lime zest, to decorate

1. Lightly grease and line a 20cm springform cake tin.

2. Put the digestive biscuits into a food processor to blitz, or use a ziplock bag and a rolling pin to gently crush the biscuits to a fine crumb. Add to a bowl with the melted butter, chopped stem ginger and salt and mix well, then press this down firmly into the base of the prepared tin, using the back of a spoon to create an even layer. Chill in the fridge whilst you make the filling.

3. Pour the cream into a large bowl and use a hand-held electric whisk to whip the cream until it forms soft peaks.

4. In another bowl use the electric whisk (no need to wash it) to beat together the cream cheese, melted white chocolate, ginger syrup and lime zest and juice. Once evenly mixed, gently fold in the whipped cream and pour this on to the chilled biscuit base. Chill in the fridge for at least 4 hours until firm.

5. To serve, carefully remove the cheesecake from the tin and top with freshly grated lime zest.

NOTES
· This will keep for up to 1 week in the fridge, making it a perfect dessert to make a few days in advance!

· Cheesecake freezes really well. Put ready-sliced sections in an airtight container, separated by greaseproof paper, and freeze for up to 3 months. Defrost in the fridge before serving.

Serves 4

I'm not a fan of pineapple on pizza, but griddled pineapple is another story – sweet and sticky with a touch of kick from the ginger and tang from the lime. This packs so much flavour that it works brilliantly with a simple good-quality vanilla ice cream, although honeycomb or salted caramel work well too!

Griddled maple and brown sugar pineapple with vanilla ice cream Ⓥ ⒼⒻ

1 medium ripe pineapple
2 tbsp maple syrup
1 tbsp soft light brown sugar
Pinch of ground ginger
Zest and juice of 2 limes, plus lime
   wedges to serve
1 tbsp butter
Small handful of fresh basil and
   mint leaves, to decorate
Vanilla ice cream, to serve

1. Prepare the pineapple by removing the top and tail with a sharp knife and then cutting away the tough skin on the sides so you're just left with the pineapple flesh. Use a pineapple corer and then cut into circles, or cut the pineapple in half lengthways and then into wedges, removing the core from each wedge.

2. Make the marinade by mixing the maple syrup, brown sugar, ground ginger, lime zest and juice together in a bowl. Pour into a ziplock bag, add the pineapple flesh and leave to marinate for at least 20 minutes and up to 4 hours.

3. Place a griddle pan over a high heat. Lightly brush the pan with the butter to stop the pineapple sticking. Add the pineapple, reserving the marinade, and griddle for 2 minutes on each side until golden and charred.

4. Scatter over a few torn basil and mint leaves. Serve with vanilla ice cream, lime wedges and a drizzle of the reserved marinade.

NOTES

· Save any leftovers to have for breakfast the next day – it's delicious on top of yoghurt or granola, or thrown into fruit salads.

· Store the cooked pineapple in an airtight container for up to 2 days.

· To make this vegan and dairy free, use coconut oil to griddle the pineapple and serve with coconut ice cream (or another dairy-free alternative).

Makes 9 doughnuts

Light, zesty and airy – not words often associated with doughnuts! Whilst I love the occasional real deal, I don't have a deep-fat fryer at home and this baked version offers all the flavour without the mess or extra kitchen equipment. They also look beautiful!

Baked lemon and poppy seed glazed doughnuts ⓥ

120g plain flour
1 tsp baking powder
½ tsp bicarbonate of soda
½ tsp salt
1 tbsp poppy seeds
60g caster sugar
30g butter, melted
60ml natural yoghurt
60ml milk
Zest and juice of 1 lemon
1 tsp vanilla bean paste (or use
    vanilla extract)
1 large egg

FOR THE GLAZE
120g icing sugar
½ tsp vanilla bean paste (or use
    vanilla extract)
Juice of 1 lemon
Toasted desiccated coconut, for
    the topping (optional)

1. Preheat the oven to 200°C/180°C fan and lightly grease some non-stick doughnut trays.

2. Combine the flour, baking powder, bicarbonate of soda, salt and poppy seeds together in a bowl. In a separate bowl, mix together the sugar, melted butter, yoghurt, milk, lemon zest and juice, vanilla and egg.

3. Fold the dry ingredients into the wet until just combined, then transfer the mixture to a piping bag or ziplock bag with a corner snipped off and gently pipe the batter into the doughnut moulds.

4. Bake for 12–14 minutes until the sponge is firm and springy to touch. Leave the doughnuts to cool in the tray while you make the glaze.

5. Put the icing sugar, vanilla and lemon juice into a clean bowl and gently mix everything together with a spoon first to avoid creating a cloud of icing sugar, then use a hand-held electric whisk on a low setting to gently beat together the mixture until it's smooth, adding a tablespoon of water to loosen it if it is too firm.

6. One at a time, dunk the tops of the doughnuts into the glaze and then place them on a wire rack. Sprinkle over some toasted desiccated coconut (if using) before the icing sets.

NOTE
· Store at room temperature for up to 3 days, or freeze the unglazed doughnuts for up to 3 months.

Makes 12 buns

Nothing beats the smell of cinnamon buns filling the kitchen in the morning. These are perfect with a hot coffee after a morning walk! I'll whip them up the day before if I have friends staying over. Leaving the cinnamon buns to have their second prove in the fridge overnight allows the yeast to develop more, giving an even deeper flavour. But of course they can be made, baked and eaten the very same day! Spreading the cream cheese glaze over the buns whilst they're still warm is essential, as this is what gives them their sticky texture, even once they've completely cooled. These are probably the most technical bake in the book, but perhaps the most special.

Overnight cinnamon buns with a maple cream cheese glaze Ⓥ

225ml milk
1 tbsp active dried yeast
90g granulated sugar, plus 1 tbsp
550g strong white bread flour
1 tsp ground cinnamon
1 tsp salt
1 tsp vanilla bean paste (or use vanilla extract)
2 large eggs
75g butter, melted

FOR THE FILLING
6 tbsp butter, at room temperature
180g soft dark brown sugar
2 tbsp ground cinnamon

1. Gently warm the milk in a pan until it's 'bath-water warm', then pour into a jug and add the yeast and the tablespoon of sugar. Stir to mix and then leave to activate for 5 minutes, or until it goes foamy.

2. Put the flour, cinnamon and salt into a large bowl. In a separate bowl, combine the 90g granulated sugar, vanilla, eggs and melted butter and then pour this into the bowl of flour along with the activated yeast milk. Mix with a spoon until a dough forms.

3. Turn out on to a lightly floured surface and knead for 8–10 minutes until a smooth dough is formed and the dough is no longer sticky. Transfer this dough to a clean and lightly oiled bowl, then cover with cling film and leave to rise in a warm place for about 1 hour, or until doubled in size. Meanwhile, grease and line a 30 x 20cm baking tray with non-stick baking paper.

4. Without disturbing the risen dough too much, roll it out on a lightly floured surface to a large rectangle, about 40 x 60cm. Spread the softened butter all over the dough rectangle, leaving an unbuttered 1cm border on all sides. Mix the sugar and cinnamon together and sprinkle this all over the dough, using your fingers to press it into the butter.

5. Starting at a long edge, tightly roll the dough up like a Swiss roll, pinching at the end to seal and keep a tight roll. Use a very sharp knife to score and then cut the roll into 12 slices, each about 4cm thick. Trim off any loose ends.

6. Place the rolls in the greased baking tray, cover tightly with cling film and place in the fridge overnight, or for at least 12 hours.

7. When you are ready to bake, remove the cinnamon rolls from the fridge, uncover and allow to come to room temperature for about 1 hour. Meanwhile, preheat the oven to 200°C/180°C fan

8. Bake for 20–25 minutes until starting to turn golden around the edges and the dough is firm to touch and hollow when tapped with a wooden spoon.

FOR THE MAPLE CREAM CHEESE GLAZE
120g cream cheese
3 tbsp butter, at room temperature
75g icing sugar
1 tsp vanilla bean paste (or use vanilla extract)
4 tbsp maple syrup
pinch of salt

9. Make the cream cheese glaze by combining everything with a hand-held electric whisk in a small bowl.

10. Remove the cinnamon buns from the oven and whilst they are still warm and in the baking tray, generously spread the glaze over the top. Enjoy warm or keep for 2–3 days in an airtight container at room temperature or up to 5 days in the fridge.

NOTE
· If you have a stand mixer, use the dough hook attachment to mix and knead the dough.

· These can be frozen once baked or after the first proving; allow to defrost overnight in the fridge and then bake as above.

Makes 16 squares

My favourite traybake is the caramel slice. The ratio of shortbread to caramel to chocolate is an important factor for me (caramel the most important!). I've added cardamom and orange zest to this shortbread for a subtle spice and refreshing citrus lift to balance the sweetness, but you can experiment with other flavourings.

Cardamom and orange caramel slice

FOR THE SHORTBREAD
160g plain flour
100g soft light brown sugar
½ tsp salt
Zest of 1 orange
Seeds from 5 cardamom pods, crushed with a pestle and mortar (or use ½ tsp ground cardamom)
125g butter, melted

FOR THE CARAMEL
2 x 400g tins condensed milk
125g butter
60g sugar
60g golden syrup
Pinch of salt

FOR THE CHOCOLATE TOPPING
200g dark chocolate
1 tbsp coconut (or vegetable) oil

1. Preheat the oven to 200°C/180°C fan and grease and line a 30 x 20cm baking tray with baking paper.

2. Combine all the shortbread ingredients together in a bowl until well combined and then tip into the lined baking tray. Press down firmly with the back of a spoon so that it's as level as possible and tightly packed. Bake for 15–20 minutes until it just begins to turn lightly golden.

3. For the caramel, melt everything together in a saucepan, whisking continually for about 10 minutes. The colour should change from pale to a deeper caramel colour, but be careful not to burn the mixture. Pour the caramel on top of the baked shortbread and return to the oven for a further 15 minutes. Remove from the oven and allow to cool to room temperature.

4. For the chocolate topping, put the chocolate and coconut oil into a heatproof bowl set over a saucepan of just simmering water (making sure the bottom of the bowl doesn't touch the water.) Stir until melted, then pour over the set caramel. Allow the tray to cool to room temperature and then cover with cling film and chill in the fridge for at least 4 hours, overnight if possible.

NOTE
· Keep in the fridge for up to 5 days.

· The tablespoon of oil mixed in with the chocolate helps to prevent the chocolate 'shattering' when you slice it with a knife.

Makes 18 biscuits

These shortbread biscuits are a great way to practise your piping skills (I use this recipe to practise piping roses!). A very forgiving mix, the heat from the oven gently blends the piping together to give them a soft textured finish – even if you mess them up they'll still taste great! They also look beautiful and make the perfect gift when wrapped up.

Vanilla shortbread swirls with white chocolate and pistachio ⓥ

220g unsalted butter, softened
120g icing sugar
1 tsp vanilla bean paste (or use vanilla extract)
250g plain flour
Pinch of salt
1 tbsp milk
100g white chocolate
30g chopped pistachios
2 tbsp edible rose petals (optional)
1 tbsp granulated sugar, for sprinkling

NOTES

· You'll need a large piping nozzle for the paste – I use a Wilton 1M.

· Undipped, the shortbread will last for up to 4 weeks in an airtight container at room temperature. Once decorated, they'll last for up to 1 week in an airtight container.

· Edible rose petals are available in some supermarkets or online.

1. Preheat the oven to 200°C/180°C fan and lightly grease and line a couple of baking trays with non-stick baking paper.

2. Cream the butter, icing sugar and vanilla together using a hand-held electric whisk until well combined, then add the flour and salt and mix again. It should become a crumb-like mixture.

3. Add the milk a teaspoon at a time and beat with the electric whisk until the mixture resembles a stiff paste. Fill a piping bag fitted with a large star nozzle with the mixture and gently pipe into shapes – choose from rings, roses or fingers.

4. Chill the piped shapes in the fridge for at least 30 minutes (or flash freeze), this will help them keep their shape when they're baked.

5. Bake for 15 minutes until just golden around the edges, then transfer to a wire rack to cool completely.

6. Put the white chocolate into a heatproof bowl set over a pan of just simmering water (making sure the bottom of the bowl doesn't touch the water) and stir until melted. Dip half of each biscuit into the melted chocolate, then scatter chopped pistachios and edible rose petals (if using) over the chocolate before it sets. Put on a sheet of baking paper to dry. Finish with a light dusting of granulated sugar over the shortbread.

Makes 16 large cookies

Bondi is home to one of the world's most famous beaches, good surf, nine months of summer, great coffee culture and – most importantly – Bennett Street Dairy. A few doors from my apartment, this café always had long queues for their warm trays of giant cookies. This is my take on those soft, cakey cookies.

The best chocolate chip cookies

180g butter, at room temperature
35g soft light brown sugar
150g condensed milk
225g plain flour
1 tsp baking powder
½ tsp salt
1 tsp vanilla bean paste (or use vanilla extract)
100g dark chocolate chips (or roughly chop up bar of chocolate)

NOTES
· Keep baked cookies stored in an airtight container for up to 5 days.

· Uncooked cookie dough can be kept for up to 5 days in the fridge or in the freezer for up to 3 months. I like to roll them in a large log so that they're ready to slice 'n' bake whenever I fancy one.

1. Using a hand-held electric whisk, cream the butter, sugar, vanilla and condensed milk together in a bowl until soft and smooth.

2. Combine the flour, baking powder and salt in a separate bowl and gently stir to mix everything together, then tip this into the wet ingredients. Use a wooden spoon or clean hands to mix everything together until it forms the cookie dough base. The dough should be firm but sticky. Gently fold in the chocolate chips until they're evenly dispersed.

3. Wrap the dough in cling film and shape it into a flat disc, then chill in the fridge for at least 1 hour.

4. Just before baking, preheat the oven to 200°/180°C fan and line a couple of baking trays with non-stick baking paper.

5. Remove the dough from the fridge and unwrap. Divide it in half and repeat until you have 16 equal-sized portions. Roll each piece of dough into a ball with your hands and place on the baking trays. Bear in mind that they will expand in the oven, so leave some space between them (you might need to bake these in batches if you don't have enough baking trays).

6. Bake for about 18 minutes; they should be just turning gold on the edges and they'll look under-baked in the middle but once they cool they'll turn soft and chewy. Keep them in the oven for 2 minutes longer if you like them crunchier.

7. Remove from the oven and leave to cool a little before you pick them up or they'll fall apart!

Makes 8 thick
slices

This is the first recipe I shared online and the most visited, liked and shared across the website. Without this banana bread I doubt this book would exist. My baking aim has always been to keep it simple and leave room for creativity – and this bread embodies that. Add chocolate chips, chopped nuts or berries and bake as a loaf, cupcakes, muffins or a traybake.

Banana bread Ⓥ

220g plain flour
½ tsp baking powder
1 tsp ground cinnamon (optional)
240g soft light brown sugar
125g butter, at room temperature
2 large eggs, at room temperature
1 tsp vanilla bean paste (or use
    vanilla extract)
250g (about 3 medium) overripe
    bananas, mashed, plus 1 to top
Demerara sugar, for sprinkling

1. Preheat the oven to 190°C/170°C fan and grease and line a 900g loaf tin.

2. Sift the flour, baking powder and cinnamon (if using) together into a bowl.

3. In a separate large bowl, cream the sugar, vanilla and butter together until there are no lumps left and you have a smooth paste, then add the eggs, one at a time, until fully mixed.

4. Tip the dry ingredients in with the wet and 'fold' together until just combined, being careful not to overmix. Finally, add the mashed bananas and fold through evenly.

5. Pour the mixture into the prepared tin and top with the extra banana, thinly sliced lengthways or chopped into coins, and a sprinkle of demerara sugar. Bake for about 1 hour, or until the loaf is golden brown and nicely risen. It's ready when there's no 'wobble' in the middle and a toothpick or skewer comes out clean when inserted into the middle of the cake.

6. Remove the loaf from the oven and wait for it to completely cool before slicing.

NOTE
· Store at room temperature in an airtight container for up to 5 days or freeze for up to 3 months. Defrost thoroughly and enjoy cool or warmed up under a grill or in the toaster.

Serves 10

My absolute favourite type of cake! It has the perfect balance of spices, and I've toasted the pecans and used brown sugar for a deep, warming flavour. Using freshly grated carrots is key for a moist sponge, and the yoghurt stops it being too heavy. Finished off with lashings of maple-spiked cream cheese frosting.

Carrot cake with cream cheese frosting

200g pecans, roughly chopped
320g plain flour
2 tsp baking powder
1 tsp bicarbonate of soda
½ tsp salt
100g sultanas
2 tsp ground cinnamon
1 tsp ground ginger
¼ tsp grated nutmeg
280g brown sugar
120g granulated sugar
240ml vegetable oil
4 large eggs
125g natural yoghurt
1 tsp vanilla extract or
    bean paste
240g (about 4) carrots, freshly
    grated

FOR THE CREAM CHEESE FROSTING
450g full fat cream cheese,
    softened
120g butter, softened
520g icing sugar
2 tbsp maple syrup
1 tsp vanilla extract or bean paste
Pinch of salt

1. Preheat the oven to 200°C/180°C fan, grease and line two 23cm cake tins and line a separate baking sheet with baking paper to toast the nuts.

2. Spread the nuts on the baking sheet and toast in the oven for 5–6 minutes until golden. Set aside.

3. In a large bowl, mix together the flour, baking powder, bicarbonate of soda, salt, sultanas and spices. In a separate bowl, mix together the sugars, oil, eggs, yoghurt and vanilla. Carefully fold the wet ingredients into the dry until just mixed, then fold through the grated carrot and three-quarters of the chopped nuts.

4. Divide the mixture between the prepared tins and bake for 30–35 minutes until a skewer comes out clean when inserted into the middle of the cake. Remove from the oven and allow the cake to completely cool.

5. To make the cream cheese frosting, use a hand-held electric whisk to beat the cream cheese and butter together until smooth, then gradually add the icing sugar until fully mixed. Add the maple syrup, vanilla and a pinch of salt to cut through the sweetness. The frosting should be thick but spreadable.

6. Spread the frosting over one of the cakes, sandwiching the other on top. Pipe or spread the remaining frosting over the top and sides of the cake. Finish by scattering with the remaining toasted pecans.

NOTE
· Store frosted carrot cake in an airtight container in the fridge for up to 5 days.

· You could use toasted pecans instead of walnuts.

Makes 24 squares

Sweet, salty and caramelised. Brown sugar and vanilla give blondies their caramelised flavoured base, and here I've used both milk and chocolate chunks and finished it off with a salty, peanut butter frosting.

White chocolate blondies with salted peanut butter frosting

170g butter, softened
225g brown sugar
2tsp vanilla extract or bean paste
1 large egg
210g plain flour
100g white chocolate, chips or
   chunks
100g milk chocolate, chips or
   chunks

FOR THE FROSTING
220g unsalted butter, softened
220g smooth roasted peanut
   butter
360g icing sugar
½–1 tsp salt
½ tsp vanilla extract
1–2 tbsp milk

1. Preheat the oven to 200°C/180°C fan and grease and line a 20cm square tin.

2. Mix the butter and sugar in a bowl. Once mixed, add the vanilla and egg. Gradually fold in the flour until just combined, then stir in the chocolate chips.

3. Pour into the prepared baking tin and bake for 20–25 minutes until the blondies have just started to turn golden on top and around the edges, and a skewer comes out clean. Remove from the oven and leave them to cool completely before frosting.

4. To make the frosting, use a hand-held electric whisk to mix the butter and peanut butter until smooth. Gradually add in the icing sugar, salt and vanilla. Add 1 teaspoon of milk at a time until the frosting is thick but spreadable. Taste and add more salt if necessary. Use a spatula to spread the frosting over the blondie base before serving.

NOTES
· Store in an airtight container in the fridge for up to 5 days.

· If anyone has nut allergies, use Biscoff instead of peanut butter.

Makes 16 squares

Chocolate and raspberry is one of my favourite combinations – sweet, tart and rich. These brownies have a fudgy, soft centre and the glossy cracked top typical of a good brownie. A tip is to take them out of the oven just before they're ready and leave them to cool completely before slicing (easier said than done!).

Chocolate and raspberry brownies

180g unsalted butter
180g dark chocolate
90g plain flour
40g cocoa powder (Dutch-processed is best)
280g caster sugar
3 large eggs, at room temperature
1 tsp vanilla bean paste (or use vanilla extract)
150g raspberries, frozen and rinsed or fresh

1. Preheat the oven to 180°C/160°C fan and lightly grease and line a 20cm square tin with non-stick baking paper.

2. In a small saucepan set over a low heat, gently melt the butter and dark chocolate together, stirring to mix them. Turn off the heat just before the butter and chocolate completely melt as they will continue to melt together off the heat. Set aside so that the mixture cools slightly to room temperature.

3. Sift the flour and cocoa powder into a large bowl, then add the sugar, eggs and vanilla and mix together until just combined.

4. Pour the slightly cooled melted butter/chocolate from the saucepan into the bowl and stir until everything is mixed together. Add the raspberries, folding them through the mixture.

5. Pour into the prepared tin and level the top with the back of a spoon or spatula. Bake for 35–40 minutes. Remove from the oven when a crust has set on the top and the edges of the brownie start to come away from the sides of the tin and paper easily. The middle should still be a little wobbly. Leave to completely cool before slicing.

NOTE
· Store at room temperature in an airtight container for up to 5 days or in the freezer for up to 3 months. Defrost thoroughly and enjoy cool or warmed up under a grill.

drinks

Smoothies

When I first moved to Australia, I worked in a whole-foods café in Bondi that made the best smoothies – there would always be a queue running out the café. All of the smoothie ingredients would be ready-prepared, portioned in Tupperware and stored in the freezer so that whenever somebody ordered one, you just needed to throw the ingredients with the liquid into a blender and blitz; it would be ready in less than a minute. I've taken this idea home with me so my freezer always has a selection of smoothie-boxes ready to go.

I've listed the ingredients I would usually use but you can substitute the milks for any plant-based, dairy-free alternatives. My favourites are almond, coconut or oat milk for their flavour and natural sweetness!

Cocktails

Much like baking, I think when you spend time choosing the perfect wine or making a nice drink, you're more likely to enjoy them mindfully, rather than knock them back mindlessly. I've included a selection of my favourite cocktails, from the light and easy-to-drink gin and Moscow mule to my all-time favourite, Espresso martini.

Please drink responsibly.

Serves 1

There are so many green smoothies out there and it can be really difficult to find one that tastes delicious – they often overcompensate with sweet and sugary ingredients to mask a bitter or grassy flavour. This is my base green smoothie recipe, full of healthy fats from the avocado and almond butter to keep me full, balanced out by the sweetness from the banana. If I have some spare vegetables or extras I fancy throwing in, I'll taste it for sweetness and add an extra teaspoon of honey or maple syrup if I need to.

Green smoothie VE GF

1 frozen banana
¼ avocado
1 tbsp almond butter
Handful of spinach
250ml almond milk

1. Put everything into a blender and blitz until smooth.

NOTES

· For a protein boost add a tablespoon of unflavoured or vanilla protein powder.

· Sometimes I'll use coconut water instead of almond milk, especially if it's really warm or I've been sweating lots as it's a great source of potassium, which helps to regulate fluid balance in the body.

Serves 1

This is a great way of sneaking a serving of greens into your diet if you struggle to get your vegetables in. The sweetness from the blueberries balances out the bitterness in the spinach, which you can't taste. The yoghurt and oats give it a thick and creamy texture – this is the one I most commonly reach for at breakfast.

Blueberry smoothie Ⓥ

20g oats
60g Greek yoghurt
Handful of spinach (or use a few
    cubes of frozen spinach)
1 tbsp honey
80g frozen blueberries
125ml almond milk
Pinch of ground cinnamon

1. Put everything into a blender and blitz until smooth.

NOTES

· For a protein boost add a tablespoon of unflavoured or vanilla protein powder.

· To make this vegan or dairy free, use coconut or soya yoghurt and sub the honey with maple syrup.

· Instead of cinnamon, try a pinch of ground cardamom. It's one of my favourite spices and works really well in this smoothie.

Serves 1

Chocolate and coffee – two of my favourite things and the perfect pick-me-up if you need something substantial but not quite a full meal. If I'm doing a morning workout I'll usually whip one of these up to have an hour or two before.

Mocha smoothie VE GF

125ml strong coffee, cooled but
  still warm
2 Medjool dates, pitted
1 frozen banana
125ml coconut milk
1 tbsp drinking chocolate
Pinch of salt

1. Put the Medjool dates into a bowl, pour over the warm coffee and soak for 5 minutes – this will help them blend more easily and give them a sticky caramel texture.

2. Put everything into a blender and blitz until smooth.

NOTE
· For a protein boost add a tablespoon of unflavoured, vanilla or chocolate protein powder.

Serves 1

A creamy and refreshing smoothie; the squeeze of lime makes all the difference! This smoothie packs in nearly 20g of protein from the Greek yoghurt and peanut butter, so it's the perfect post-workout fuel.

Mango, peanut and lime smoothie **GF**

75g frozen mango
100g Greek yoghurt
2 tbsp peanut butter
1 tbsp honey
125ml coconut milk
1 ripe banana
Juice of ½ lime

1. Put everything (except the lime juice) into a blender and blitz until smooth.

2. Serve with a generous squeeze of lime juice.

NOTES

· For a protein boost add a tablespoon of unflavoured or vanilla protein powder.

· To make this vegan or dairy free, use coconut or soya yoghurt and sub the honey with maple syrup.

Serves 1

My favourite flavour combination of all time has to be salted caramel! Medjool dates add a deep caramel flavour and if I have time, I like to soak them for 5 minutes beforehand. This makes them plump, juicy and soft so they are easier to blend.

Salted caramel and date smoothie

20g oats
2 Medjool dates, pitted
1 tbsp almond butter
1 frozen banana
125ml almond milk
Pinch of salt
½ tsp vanilla bean paste (or use vanilla extract)

1. Put the pitted Medjool dates in a small cup of hot water and soak for 5 minutes.

2. Drain the softened dates (discarding the water) and add to a blender with all the other ingredients. Blitz until smooth.

NOTE
· For a protein boost add a tablespoon of unflavoured or vanilla protein powder.

Serves 2

'Wake me up and then f**k me up' are the words that led to the creation of this cocktail in the late 1980s. My favourite cocktail of all time, this equal-parts recipe makes it super-quick and easy to create. I leave out the sugar syrup that is usually used and add a dusting of crumbled honeycomb instead of coffee beans to decorate, giving a salted caramel edge.

Espresso martini ⓥ

50ml vodka
50ml fresh, hot coffee
50ml Kahlua coffee liqueur
Large handful of ice
Small handful of honeycomb,
   crumbled

1. Pour all the ingredients into a shaker with ice and shake vigorously.

2. Strain into a coupe or martini glass and garnish with the crumbled honeycomb.

NOTE
· If you can't find honeycomb, use my tip on page 34 using Crunchie bars.

Serves 2

Once I'd ditched the bright blue alcopops and vodka-diet-somethings, gin became 'my thing'. My favourite is the botanical Monkey 47, or a simple Hendricks. Gin sales in the UK increased by 56 per cent in 2019 and 247 new gin brands have entered the market in the last five years (accounting for 24 per cent of all new product development). Preferring to keep mine simple and without the colour pink or enough berries to confuse it with a Pimms, I first had this herb-infused gin in San Miguel, a quiet and rugged village tucked away on the beautiful northern coast of Ibiza.

Rosemary gin **VE**

120ml gin (I use Hendricks)
2 handfuls of ice
¼ cucumber, julienned or sliced into long ribbons
2 fresh sprigs of rosemary
240ml good-quality tonic water

1. Pour the measured gin between 2 tall glasses and add a handful of ice to each.

2. Add cucumber ribbons and fresh rosemary sprigs to each glass and top with tonic water.

Serves 2

Sweet, spicy, strong and – better yet – made with just three ingredients. My friend and I sunk a few of these on a rooftop in Vietnam, choosing to spend our hard-earned travel savings on drinks and the city view rather than a hostel for the night. We slept on the Ho Chi Minh airport floor before basing our next destination on the cheapest flight available the following morning. A simple cocktail for a simple life. As with the tonic water in a good gin and tonic, the mixer makes up three-quarters of your drink, so it's worth getting a good-quality one. Traditionally served in a copper mug but any normal glass will do!

Moscow mule **VE**

120ml vodka
2 handfuls of ice
1 lime
240ml good-quality ginger beer
Extra lime wedges, thinly sliced
    fresh ginger and mint leaves,
    to garnish

1. Pour the measured vodka between 2 tall glasses and add a handful of ice to each.

2. Roll the lime back and forth with your hand on a hard surface (this makes it easier to squeeze) before slicing in half and squeezing the juice of ½ lime into each glass.

3. Top up with the ginger beer and swirl gently with the back of a spoon. Garnish each glass with an extra wedge of lime, thinly sliced fresh ginger and mint leaves.

NOTE
· Try a Mexican (tequila) or Jamaican (rum) version.

Serves 2

This classic cocktail was allegedly inspired by the drinkers in 1800s' Kentucky, who refused to change and ordered their drinks 'the old-fashioned' way: dark spirit, water dissolved in sugar and bitters. Traditionally served in a short tumbler 'rocks' glass with citrus rind and a maraschino cherry. Rich, silky and smooth.

Old fashioned

1 tsp sugar
2 tsp water
4 dashes of Angostura bitters
2 orange slices
2 handfuls of ice
120ml whiskey (bourbon or rye)
2 strips of orange peel, to garnish
2 maraschino cherries, to garnish

1. Divide the sugar, water and Angostura bitters between 2 chilled glasses and mix together with a muddler until the sugar has dissolved. Rotate each glass so this evenly coats the bottom and sides, then add an orange slice to each and gently muddle again.

2. Add the ice to the glasses, then pour over the whiskey, giving it another gentle stir. Garnish each with the orange peel and a maraschino cherry.

Serves 2

A velvety cacao and cream base dusted with nutmeg make this my ideal 'dessert cocktail'. I first had (and fell in love with) this in Australia's capital, Canberra, in the middle of winter in front of a roaring open fire. I've since had it as a 'spiked milkshake' swapping double cream for ice cream – which was equally delicious!

Brandy Alexander

90ml cognac
50ml creme de cacao
50ml double cream
Large handful of ice
Freshly grated nutmeg, to garnish

1. Pour all the ingredients into a shaker with the ice and shake vigorously.

2. Strain into a coupe or cocktail glass and garnish with freshly grated nutmeg.

Index

HarperCollins*Publishers*
1 London Bridge Street
London SE1 9GF

www.harpercollins.co.uk

HarperCollins*Publishers*
1st Floor, Watermarque Building, Ringsend Road
Dublin 4, Ireland

First published by HarperCollins*Publishers* 2021

4

Text © Lucy Lord 2021
Photography © HarperCollins*Publishers* 2021

Lucy Lord asserts the moral right to be
identified as the author of this work

A catalogue record of this book is available
from the British Library

ISBN 978-0-00-842108-3

Photographer: Faith Mason
Food Stylist: Pippa Leon
Prop Stylist: Alexander Breeze

Printed and bound in Latvia

MIX
Paper from
responsible sources
FSC™ C007454

FSC
www.fsc.org

This book is produced from independently certified FSC™ paper
to ensure responsible forest management.

For more information visit: www.harpercollins.co.uk/green

Acknowledgements

Thank you to everybody at HarperCollins
who has helped bring my book to life.
Lydia, Sarah, Harriet, Hattie and James.
Thank you so much for your hard work
and creativity. Thank you to Alex for the
prop styling, to Pippa and Sian who styled
the food so beautifully and to Faith for
capturing it.

A special thank you to Luke for your
selfless hard work, kindness and for
always seeing the bigger picture. Thank
you James for making everything more
fun and for never saying no to a home
bake. To my mum and dad for always
welcoming me into their kitchen and,
moreover, for always being there to
clean up the mess. Thank you, Steph,
for everything.

Finally, my deepest gratitude to you, the
reader. Whether you're new to the kitchen
or would spend all your days there if given
the option. Your support means more
than I can put into words. Thank you.

Create, share, make a mess and then
start all over again – it's good for the soul.